A Year of Teatime Tales

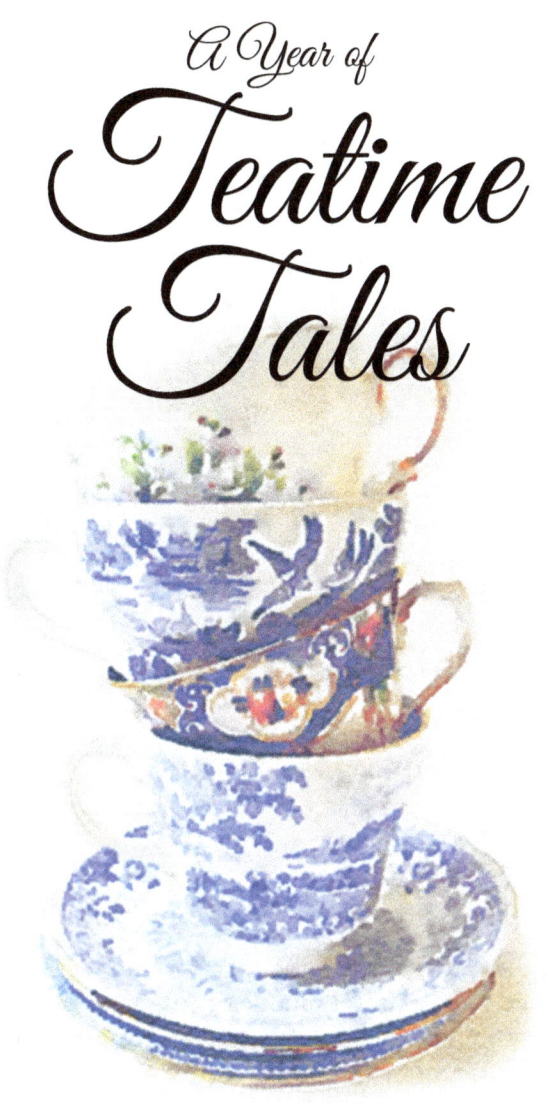

52 tea-themed stories to
fill your cup and warm your heart

Angela Webster McRae

Copyright © 2016 Angela Webster McRae
Published in the United States of America.
Written and photographed by Angela Webster McRae.
Design by Deberah Williams.

ISBN # 978-0-692-66513-8

Acknowledgments

If my tea-blogger friend Judith Rogers of Ontario (lavendercottagegardening.com) hadn't blogged about her new Waterlogue app one day early in 2014, I'm not sure I would have ever been inspired to tackle a yearlong project of writing tea-themed short stories on my Tea With Friends blog (teawithfriends.blogspot.com). I needed some artwork that would merely suggest the subject of each story, and this amazing app on my iPad turned my photos into watercolor-ish images that did the trick. I will always be grateful to Judith for the inspiration!

To my loyal Tea With Friends blog readers—including my most loyal and supportive reader ever, my husband, Alex—thank you for following along on my whimsical year of fictionalizing teacups and teapots and tea parties. It was incredibly rewarding to hear that so many of you looked forward to my weekly stories, and it was even more rewarding to be asked to compile them into a book. It was also because of my blog readers that one particularly well-received story, "The Women's Ministry Committee Meeting for the 42nd Annual Spring Tea," was expanded into a series of four stories about the tea lady who famously got her feelings hurt when her tea sandwich recipe wasn't chosen for the church tea.

I am also grateful to those who gave me the many treasured teawares featured in this book's artwork. The "I Heart Tea" travel mug on page 171 came from my sister, Rhonda Horton. My friend Norma Haynes gave me the Shelley sugar and creamer on page 187 as a wedding gift. My friend Liz Barnett gifted me with a sentimental favorite, one of her grandmother's teacups and saucers, which inspired the story on page 39. My friend Katherine McCall met me on the porch of a tearoom and surprised me with the marvelous Chinese tea basket and teawares on page 83. And my tea-loving New York pen pal, Sandy Maniscalco, probably had no idea I would be using one of her many letters for the artwork on page 99, but I was lucky to have it. I am so fortunate to have friends and family who indulge my love of teatime.

And as always, I thank my talented friend Deberah Williams for the skill and grace she brings to every design project I've ever asked her to tackle, including the design of this book. Thank you for always making me look better than I am, and may we enjoy many more projects together over many more cups of tea!

Table of Contents

1. New Year's Resolutions ... 7
2. Tempest in a Tea Cabinet ... 11
3. Put a Lid On It ... 15
4. The Women's Ministry Committee Meeting for the 42nd Annual Spring Tea ... 19
5. Outbid! ... 23
6. Shattered ... 27
7. A Friendly Valentine ... 31
8. A Taste of Wisdom ... 35
9. The Silverdale Dishes ... 39
10. On Kindness and Carrots ... 43
11. The Legend of the Shamrock Teacup ... 47
12. A Growing Friendship ... 51
13. The Rhinestone Teapot Pin ... 55
14. A Cup of Easter Tea ... 59
15. Taking Tea with the Methodists ... 63
16. She Dreams in Roses ... 67
17. The Japanese Tea Set ... 71
18. Teatime with Aunt Eleanor ... 75
19. The Mother's Day Tea Mug ... 79
20. The Chinese Tea Basket ... 83
21. Memories and Memorial Day ... 87
22. The Secret Diary of a Garden Party Attendee ... 91
23. The Mostly True Story of Shen Nung ... 95
24. The Pleasure of a Letter ... 99
25. Times Remembered ... 103

26	The Vintage Iced Tea Pitcher	107
27	Tomato Sandwich Freedom Day	111
28	Just Because	115
29	Power to the Pot	119
30	Teatime in Paradise	123
31	Planning for the Ladies Guild Fall Tea	127
32	First Day of School	131
33	The Whisper	135
34	Those Tea Party Pinkies	139
35	A Nutty Dessert	143
36	I Will Always Love You	147
37	Plain, Reliable Betty	151
38	Art and Inspiration	155
39	A Prize-Winning Quilt	159
40	A Cup of Hope	163
41	The Blossom	167
42	Just Say No	171
43	Teapot Ella	175
44	Time Change	179
45	High Tea	183
46	Knickknacks	187
47	A Family Thanksgiving	191
48	Lunching at the Swan Coach House	195
49	"Ho, ho, ho! Merry Christmas!"	199
50	The Baptists and Christmas Tea	203
51	Tea on Christmas Morning	207
52	A Year of Teatime	211

A Year of Teatime Tales

1
New Year's Resolutions

Sitting in front of her living room fireplace on New Year's Day, Marsha opened the pretty red leather journal and uncapped a matching fountain pen. Where to begin?

Every year she made a list of New Year's Resolutions.

Every year she fully intended to accomplish them.

Every year she failed at most of them. This past year she hadn't learned French, she hadn't lost ten pounds, and she hadn't even managed to keep up with her daily two-mile walk. Something always seemed to come up to thwart her good intentions.

Closing the journal, Marsha decided to postpone making the new year's to-do list until after she finished packing up the Christmas decorations. She'd taken the Christmas tree down the day before, but boxes of ornaments were still sitting in a spare bedroom. Now that Katie's family had gone home, there was no reason to keep all those stuffed Santas and elves out.

Katie, Marsha and Rick's only child, had driven up to Tennessee from Florida with her two-year-old daughter, Olivia, in mid-December. Marsha had so enjoyed having them there before the holiday rush set in. Katie's husband, Josh, had arrived a few days before Christmas after finally taking a break from the tech company where he worked. His job had something to do with website security. Marsha didn't really understand it, she just knew that Josh was successful enough for Katie to be a full-time homemaker just as Marsha had always been.

On Christmas Day, Marsha and Rick got a surprise after Olivia woke up from her afternoon nap. Katie walked in with a mischievous grin and said Olivia wanted to model a new outfit for them.

"Mom, Dad, what do you think of Olivia's T-shirt?" Katie had asked.

Marsha thought it was an odd question until Olivia twirled around in her glittery Christmas tutu and long-sleeved white T-shirt that read, "I'm going to be a Big Sister!"

There were tears and hugs all around as Katie revealed she and Josh were expecting a little boy in the summer.

Day One of the new year, and already Marsha knew it would be a good one.

Right now, though, she had a major case of post-holiday disorganization and was eager to get her house back in order.

Rick was busy watching bowl games back in his Man Cave, and that was fine by her. Marsha went into the kitchen and removed her Christmas planner from the shelf that housed all her cookbooks. Each year she wrote down where she stored the various decorations. If it was the year for red and green decorations, she'd know that these were stored in the garage. If it was the year for the Shabby Chic tree with the white and pink decorations, which Rick didn't really care for, she'd know that these were up in the attic. Katie had loved that pink tree when she was a teenager, but Rick insisted it wasn't really a Christmas tree if it didn't have red and green on it.

Marsha smiled as she reflected on how many Christmases she and Rick had enjoyed in this house. It was where they had raised their daughter, and now it was where they got to enjoy the holidays with their adorable granddaughter. Soon, a grandson would be part of their celebrations too.

After Marsha jotted down a few more details about Christmas decorations, she decided to make a cup of tea. Katie and Josh had given her an Old Country Roses teapot and four matching cups and saucers for Christmas. It was too extravagant a gift, she told them. They shouldn't have spent so much. With a small child and another on the way, surely they needed to save their money.

Yet Marsha loved her new teapot. She had always admired Old Country Roses but had never owned a piece of it. Now, she had the teapot and enough teacups to have three friends over as well.

"Katie, Josh, you shouldn't have," Marsha said when she opened her gift. "It's too much."

"Mom," Katie had said, "just enjoy it, okay? You worry too much. If we couldn't afford it, we wouldn't do it, would we?"

Marsha hadn't wanted to seem ungrateful, so she let it go.

In fact, she was learning to let a lot of things go.

Marsha thought about her daughter's words as she spooned some loose leaf tea into her new teapot. After the kettle on the stovetop whistled, she filled the teapot and gazed out the window as the tea steeped for four minutes.

Rick walked in to get a snack during halftime of one of his ballgames.

"What are you studying so hard?" he asked.

"Hmm? Oh, nothing. Just putting up the last of the decorations and working on my list of New Year's resolutions."

"Who needs the pressure of another to-do list?" Rick said. "I'm making a nice big to-don't list for the new year," he joked, heading off with a bag of chips and some salsa.

A to-don't list. Rick's words lingered in her mind.

When the timer sounded, Marsha poured herself a fragrant cup of Earl Grey and carried the Old Country Roses teacup and saucer to the living room, careful not to spill any tea as she curled up on the sofa.

Marsha thought about what her daughter had said, that she worried too much. And she thought about what Rick had just asked, who needed the pressure of another to-do list?

Why did she? Marsha realized she had much to be thankful for: a loving husband, a great daughter and son-in-law, a precious granddaughter, and soon, a new grandson to spoil. Maybe she should simply focus on her blessings this year.

Placing her teacup and saucer on an ottoman, Marsha opened her new journal and carefully wrote across the top of a page, "To Do Not."

#1. Worry.

#2. Obsess over a list of New Year's Resolutions.

She smiled, closed her journal, capped her pen, and slowly sipped a delicious cup of tea.

2
Tempest in a Tea Cabinet

Rose was having a bad day. She felt old and tired, she wasn't appreciated by anyone anymore, and to top it all off, the winter blues had her in an ill humor. Thank goodness her friend Gracie had time to listen to her.

"It's the same thing, time after time," Rose whined. "They love us when we're young and pretty, and then time catches up to us, or a newer model comes along, and bam, they shove us aside and go in search of someone more exciting."

Gracie could only nod in agreement. She hated to see her friend in such a foul mood, but she knew that what Rose was saying was true: It was hard being a teacup.

"I know what you mean," said Gracie. "Or at least I've heard about that kind of thing."

Gracie, who was from China, wasn't that old herself, three years at the most. Rose, on the other hand, had come to America from England in the 1950s, and her age was starting to show. She had no cracks and no chips, but the faintest little lines were beginning to appear on her saucer, and some of the gold on her rim and handle had disappeared—along with her youth.

"I don't know why I'm even talking to you about this," Rose said. "You're practically a baby. The mistress still thinks you're the cat's meow."

"But Rose, you *know* she loves you," Gracie said. "Doesn't she tell people that the fact you're a little crazy—I mean 'crazed,' of course—is one of the best things about you?"

"Phooey," said Rose. "She says it, but she doesn't mean it."

Gracie sighed. "Of course she does. I think you've just got a bad case of the winter blahs, or blues, or whatever they call them."

"It's blues, sweetie," Rose said, just a trifle dismissively. "But I am not imagining this. Look over there by that electric teakettle. Who's she got out there today? That same old ivory creamware cup and saucer she falls in love with every single January."

Perhaps, Gracie thought, she should try playing peacemaker. "Now, Rose, Creamy likes to get outside this cabinet just as much as the rest of us. And really, does she ever get to go out and play any time besides January? I don't think so. At least the rest of us get a turn all year long."

"You're missing the point, Gracie," said Rose. "I just don't see why Creamy gets all the attention every January. Oh sure, her handle's pretty, but everything else about her is plain, plain, plain. Bor-ing, and the other thing—"

"Rose," said Gracie, a little more firmly, "I don't see what good it does to complain. You're a teacup, not the mistress of the house. Don't you think it's time to let it go?" Gracie started to hum the "Let It Go" song from the Disney movie *Frozen*, and Rose wanted to scream, but she couldn't, because she was a teacup—and teacups were far too polite to scream.

Undeterred, Rose continued. "As I was going to say before I was so rudely interrupted, the other thing that bugs me is how our mistress always talks about how gray and dull it is each January, but then what does she do to put a little color in her life? She reaches for a beige teacup! It makes no sense."

Gracie had had just about enough of Rose's bad attitude. "Fine," she said. "If you want to sit here all day and stew over it, suit yourself. I'm going to take a nap and think about how much fun I'm going to have when she pulls me back out in the spring."

"If," said Rose.

"What?" asked Gracie.

"IF she pulls you back out in the spring," Rose said, giving Gracie a knowing, condescending smile.

"Oh, Rose ..."

Gracie closed her eyes, settled down into her saucer, and got ready for a nice long winter's nap. In fact, she so enjoyed her nap that the next morning, it frightened her when the cabinet door suddenly whipped open at seven a.m. What was going on?

It was the mistress, and she was rummaging around among the stacks of teacups.

"Ouch," whispered Gracie, whose saucer was shoved around in the course of the search. Gracie didn't like to be jerked out of her sleep.

"I know you're in here somewhere," said the mistress. "Ah, there you are!"

The comment caused Gracie to open her eyes wide. The mistress was reaching for ... Rose!

"That beige teacup doesn't have enough personality. I need a little color to brighten this day, and I think you're just the one to bring it, sweet friend." The mistress shoved the other teacups aside, slid the creamware set into the spot Rose had occupied, and shut the cabinet door.

Gracie peered out the cabinet's glass to see what was going on with Rose. The mistress was filling her with boiling water, and Gracie soon caught the slightest

A Year of Teatime Tales

whiff of vanilla through a crack in the door.

So Rose was wanted once more.

And none too soon.

Gracie closed her eyes, snuggled back down into her saucer, and returned to the land of slumbering teacups.

3
Put a Lid On It

It's another snowy morning here in Cleveland, Ohio, as good a time as any to sort through that box of stuff that belonged to Grandma Prescott. I'm still unsure why Mom gave it to me. There are some old letters Grandpa wrote to Grandma during World War II. We're lucky Grandpa came back since so many men didn't. Think I'll set those letters aside to read this afternoon.

Here's one of those cardinal figurines Grandma used to collect. She did love her pretty red birds.

What's in this old pillowcase? I don't remember seeing this when Mom gave me the box. A tarnished silver teapot. Hmm. The lid doesn't come off. Oh, it's got a hinge. Guess you'll never misplace the lid that way. What does it say on the bottom? "The Heery Brothers Tearoom." Hey, that's the old tearoom where Grandma worked when she first met Grandpa. Or at least I think that's what

Mom always said. I'll have to ask her about that next time we talk. I wonder why Grandma kept this old teapot?

Alice Fay Davidson loved her job at the Heery Brothers Department Store Tearoom in Cleveland. She'd worked there a year now, hired the same week she graduated from high school in 1942.

Heery Brothers was Cleveland's most upscale department store. Women were eager to work there for many reasons, not least of which was the employee discount. Alice liked knowing she could always afford a new scarf or blouse each payday, proudly taking each new purchase home in one of the store's famous shopping bags with salmon-colored geraniums on them.

The other reason Alice enjoyed her job was that like most nineteen-year-old women, she was eager to get married and start a family, and a lot of handsome men shopped at Heery's. She had dated the boys in high school, but that was the problem—they were just boys. Alice was looking for a *man*.

One Wednesday afternoon, some time between taking Cobb Salads to two ladies at Table Three and delivering the check to a mother and toddler at Table One, Alice saw a man at Table Four who nearly made her drop her order pad. She was about to place it back in her apron pocket when she glanced up and saw the man in uniform boldly watching her. He didn't even try to hide his interest.

Alice quickly looked away, but she couldn't forget that face. Those eyes.

She headed to the kitchen to pick up another order, and when she got there, Blanche Monroe, the manager, whistled at her.

"What's that for?" Alice asked.

"Don't pretend you didn't notice the good-looking Air Force guy at Table Four," Blanche said. "We all think he looks like a young Nelson Eddy. You should go after him."

Alice laughed. "Don't be silly. Men like that have more

girls than they can shake a stick at. I think he just wants a hot meal, that's all."

"Sure," Blanche said. "If you say so."

Alice had to admit the man was good-looking. She composed herself before going over to take his order.

"Hi, I'm Alice." A blush rose on her cheeks. "Can I get you something to drink?"

"I'll have a small pot of tea," he said. "By the way, I'm Frank Prescott."

"We don't usually have men order tea here," Alice said. "Most men order coffee."

"My mother was British, so I grew up drinking tea," Frank said. "Old habits die hard."

"Well, that explains it then," Alice said, smiling a little more than she meant to. "I'll be right back with your tea."

Filling one of the small silver teapots in the kitchen, Alice was grilled by Blanche and her fellow waitresses.

"What did he say?"

"What's his name?"

"Where's he from?"

But Alice didn't have time to waste. She took Frank's tea to his table and poured him a cup before taking his lunch order of Almond Rarebit, a popular cheese and toast dish. No one joined him for lunch, and when she took him the check at the completion of his meal, he was extra friendly, telling her he was in town on business from Wright Field over in Dayton.

"How long have you worked here?" Frank asked.

"A year. I couldn't decide whether to go to secretarial school or not, so I thought working here would help me earn some money while I decide where I want to go in life."

"I've got an idea of where you can go," Frank said, his blue eyes twinkling.

"Oh, really?"

"Yes, there's a great new band playing over at the country club Friday night, and I'm invited and can bring a date. I think we'd have a swell time. Unless ..."

"Unless what?"

"Unless you've got a fellow."

"No, I don't," Alice said. "And thanks. I'd like that."

Frank pulled out a small notepad and pen. He asked Alice for her phone number and address and said he'd see her at seven p.m. Friday.

"It was nice meeting you," she said as he rose to leave. Out of the corner of her eye, she saw two of the waitresses watching them.

"You too, Alice. And by the way, that's some of the best tea I've ever had. You make it nice and strong here, just like my mother always did. Or maybe you've got a magic teapot. Is that it?"

"Could be," Alice said. "You'll have to come back and try it again another day."

Blanche, who had suddenly decided she needed to refresh the flowers on Table One, overheard the whole conversation.

"Give me that teapot," she told Alice once Frank left.

"Why?"

"I'm putting it up on the shelf and saving it for your wedding gift. You're going to marry that man."

"Don't be ridiculous, Blanche. You can't know something like that."

"Just hand me the teapot and put a lid on it, will you?"

4
The Women's Ministry Committee Meeting for the 42nd Annual Spring Tea

Catholics, I am told, believe in the doctrine of Purgatory, an intermediate state after death where the heaven-bound undergo purification in order to achieve holiness before entering heaven. Southern Baptists have something similar, only we call it the Women's Ministry Committee Meeting for the Annual Spring Tea.

Starla Mooneyham has called the meeting this fine Saturday morning in January so we can decide on the menu for our 42nd Annual Spring Tea. The Spring Tea is second in importance only to the Second Coming at my church. Women

A Year of Teatime Tales

pull out their best china and set a table in springtime pastels. We're supposed to do this because we love the Lord and want to reach The Unchurched, but the truth of the matter is that some women—looking at you, Eloise Wilson—like to show off their table-setting skills and family linens.

Starla knows that I, Brenda Johnson, am the president of the local tea society, so I'm sure that's why she invited me to be on the committee again. Ten of us were asked to prepare a tray of our favorite tea sandwiches, and today we'll choose five of them to serve at the Spring Tea.

Now I didn't have to think twice about what to make. Friends always rave about my Waldorf Chicken Salad on Mini Croissants, so I whipped up a bowl of chicken salad last night and made the sandwiches this morning. I don't like to brag, but I've basically perfected this recipe, so I'm sure it'll be chosen. I almost feel sorry for the other ladies since not all of us can have our sandwiches selected, but what can I say? I've been making tea sandwiches a long time. I will not apologize for that.

Starla calls the meeting to order and asks Ann Simpson to pray. I wish she had called on someone else. Ann believes in informational praying, the kind where the pray-er feels that she has to give God a news update on the pray-ee. "And Lord, we ask you to be with Carolyn, because she couldn't be here today since her sinuses are acting up again. Dear Lord, we just thank You that You can solve her sinus problems and work on that unspoken marital need of hers all at once, dear Lord." After what seems like an eternity, Ann decides to wind things up, and we all gather round to sample tea sandwiches.

I don't eat one of my own sandwiches, of course, because that would be tacky. Instead, I double up on Mary Lou Carter's pimiento cheese sandwiches. Mary Lou can hardly boil water, bless her heart, and you do *not* want that woman making a thing for the fall bake sale. I'll tell you that right now. But Mary Lou makes the best pimiento cheese of all of us, a fact I find no less miraculous than Jesus turning the water into wine.

Marcia Brown brought some cucumber sandwiches she cut out with a cute little flower-shaped cookie cutter.

They taste fine, but a plain old cucumber and cream cheese sandwich isn't very imaginative, in my humble opinion.

Starla offered to make the tea for our sandwich tasting, which I knew meant she'd bring some off-brand from the dollar store. I cannot seem to convince these women of the importance of using quality loose leaf tea. Starla wouldn't know quality tea if it jumped out of the tea tin and slapped her upside the head, but she's the one leading the ladies this year, so I don't say anything. As usual, I just keep my opinions to myself.

After about thirty minutes, we're all through eating sandwiches. Ann notes that the group has always voted on the sandwiches by secret ballot. Starla, however, wants us to discuss our favorites openly and agree on the selections. That suits me fine, but I don't know how some of the ladies will take it when theirs aren't chosen.

I am not at all surprised when Starla points to the tray with my sandwiches—or what used to be my sandwiches, since only one is left. I'm accustomed to this. She picks it up and says, "These tasted great, but they're a bit large for the luncheon plates. We'd probably need to cut them in half, and I'm sure Brenda would rather we not do that. So thanks for bringing these, but I think we need to go with some smaller sandwiches."

To say that I am stunned is an understatement. Does Starla not understand that women *love* my Waldorf Chicken Salad Mini Croissants? Is she unaware that my recipe once appeared in *Southern Lady* magazine? Where does she get off saying my mini croissants are too big, anyway? Who died and made her the tea sandwich queen?

"Brenda, do you agree?"

I quickly realize I've missed something. "Sorry. I was busy thinking about what I'm cooking for Sunday dinner tomorrow. Could you repeat that?"

"We just wanted to see if you like Marcia's cucumber sandwiches as much as everyone else does. They seem to be the favorites."

"Yes, they're very good," I say, forcing a smile. *Very good if you don't mind a boring, overused, underimagined tea sandwich that looks like a third grader assembled it.*

"Great," says Starla. She adds cucumber sandwiches to the list that also includes Mary Lou's pimiento cheese sandwiches, Starla's own egg salad triangles—which I personally find a little low-rent for teatime, but I don't say anything—and two sliced fruit sandwiches, apple and strawberry, that just *happen* to have been made by Starla's two best friends. Nobody ever serves two fruit sandwiches at a tea.

But I don't care. Like I say, I always keep my opinions to myself. If these women want to behave like a bunch of teatime amateurs, why should I care?

I've been thinking of becoming a Methodist anyway. I wonder if they have a Spring Tea?

5

Outbid!

Laura told herself not to get her hopes up. She had wanted one of those lovely old-fashioned tablecloths for years. She had never learned to crochet as both of her sisters had, so instead she prowled flea markets, yard sales, and eBay, looking for pretty old linens since she didn't know how to make them herself.

A few years ago, she was searching eBay when she'd come across the prettiest tablecloth ever. Pristine white and made of fine linen, the cloth was an elegant square trimmed in a filet crochet edging that depicted a teapot, teacups, and sugar and creamer. In mint condition, it was the prettiest teatime tablecloth Laura had ever seen. Unfortunately, the eBay buyers thought so, too, and got into a bidding war over it. The price ultimately shot up to more than a hundred dollars, so Laura didn't win it. Ever since, she'd watched eBay, looking for a similar tablecloth.

A week ago, Laura got an alert from eBay in her morning e-mail noting that another of those beautiful tablecloths had just been listed. She was thrilled. This time, she was not going to let the tablecloth get away. Still, she knew she needed to exercise caution.

"Just because that pretty tablecloth showed up on eBay doesn't mean it's mine," she told herself. "Every tea lover out there seems to want one of these. Sure, it's got the filet crochet edging of teapots and teawares that I've been trying to find for years, but that still doesn't mean it's mine. I won't get too attached to it until I win the bid."

Laura had often wondered why she was so attracted to old linens. Maybe it was because they were vintage. Maybe it was because of the delicate needlework. Maybe it was because she liked to imagine the woman who once made the piece. And maybe it was a bit of all of that.

Laura had been watching the tablecloth auction on eBay for a solid week, and no one had even placed an opening bid of $19.99. In her mind, it was already "her" tablecloth, and she had a hunch the bidding would turn out differently this time.

The auction went off at 3:16 p.m. on Friday, and by 2:16 that afternoon, she was in the living room, staring at the laptop screen in front of her. Watching. Waiting. She couldn't wait to win "her" tablecloth.

At a quarter till three, there were still no bids. Then, at 3:01, they started to appear. First came the $19.99 bid. Then the price of the tablecloth quickly shot up to $25.99, then $27.99, and $29.99. Soon, the bid was $44.99, and then $57.99. Laura did not like the turn the bidding had taken.

The bidding was already at $86.99, and there were thirteen minutes left in the auction. When the bid got up to $101.99 with ten minutes left, Laura closed her laptop, sighed, and went into the kitchen, where she made herself a cup of plum-flavored tea. Clearly, she wasn't meant to have this tablecloth.

It had been two years since she last saw one of these gorgeous cloths listed on eBay. At this rate, it could be another two years before one even came up for auction again.

Maybe she just needed to learn how to crochet and make her own tablecloth with the fancy crocheted edging.

But no, that would never work. She didn't like to stay indoors very long, and once gardening season arrived, she would be outside separating the irises and pruning the rose bushes. It was time to forget the tablecloth and move on.

The next morning, Laura decided to stop by her Aunt Carolyn's house before going grocery shopping.

"Hey, hon," Carolyn said. "Come on in and have a cup of tea." Her aunt could always be counted on to offer a cup of tea.

Laura headed into her aunt's kitchen to turn on the stovetop teakettle, and her aunt walked up behind her and handed her a wadded-up Walmart bag.

"What's this?"

"Just something I found at a yard sale yesterday. Looked like the kind of old linens you like," she said, heading back to the living room.

While Laura waited for the water to boil, she looked in the bag and couldn't believe what she saw.

"Aunt Carolyn!" she called in the direction of the living room. "Where did you find this?"

"Got it at that yard sale off First Street yesterday," she said. "Why? Don't you like it?"

Laura unfolded the pristine white square of fine linen and studied the immaculately crocheted edging of a teapot, teacups, and sugar and creamer.

"Oh no, I absolutely love it," Laura said. "Truly, I love it."

"Good," Carolyn said. "I paid three dollars for it. You don't think that's too much, do you?"

"Oh no," Laura called back. "I don't think that's too much at all."

"Glad to hear it," Carolyn said. "I figured if nothing else, you could sell it on eBay and get a few dollars for it. I hear people pay outrageous prices for some of that junk on there."

"So I hear, Aunt Carolyn," Laura said, still fingering the beautiful, lacy edging. "So I hear."

6
Shattered

There was always something about that boy that Ellen hadn't liked.

The day Sarah Grace came home with Josh, Ellen told her husband, "Ed, I'm worried about this one. Sarah Grace has a certain look on her face when she's around him and when she talks about him. I've never seen that look before, and there's something about that boy that doesn't seem right."

Ed said, for the thousandth time, that she was imagining things. After what happened last week, he knew she had been right, but it was small comfort to her.

Josh had asked Sarah Grace to marry him last year on the Fourth of July, and she accepted. Their wedding was supposed to have been a romantic, over-the-top, all-pink extravaganza set for Valentine's Day, but Josh broke up with her the night of the Super Bowl. He sent her a text from Arizona and said

being with his buddies made him realize he wasn't ready for marriage. He was breaking it off, as he put it, "because I think it's best for both of us."

Sarah Grace was understandably devastated. While a part of Ellen was glad her daughter wouldn't be marrying any boy stupid enough to leave her, Ellen's heart was breaking for her little girl.

Sarah Grace was twenty-five and plenty old enough to be getting married, but to Ellen, her only child would always be her little girl. Ellen absolutely despised having to watch Sarah Grace live through the humiliation and hurt of a broken engagement.

Her daughter returned to the classroom the Tuesday after the ballgame. Ellen knew Sarah Grace would teach her heart out to that class of third graders just as she always had, heartbreak or no heartbreak.

Ellen still could not believe Josh broke up with Sarah Grace less than two weeks before their wedding.

Ed continued to stew over all the money he'd lost, which Ellen thought was just like a man. He threatened, "I'm going to send Josh's family a bill for the wedding dress, the caterer, the photographer ..."

"You'll do no such thing," Ellen said. "Consider it money well spent for getting that boy out of our lives."

Ed didn't see it that way, but he hadn't said any more about it.

Ellen, however, kept thinking about Sarah Grace and how hard the past two days had been for her. It wasn't easy to call your best friend and seven other bridesmaids to tell them those three-hundred-dollar pink organza dresses would not be worn on February 14 after all. Ellen took care of as much of the unpleasantness as she could, but she quickly learned that some things simply couldn't be undone. Wedding invitations couldn't be unsent. Gifts of wedding china couldn't be unopened. A photographer couldn't be unbooked, but at least this one said his deposit could be applied to any future nuptials.

Ellen knew that her aggravation was nothing compared to the heartbreak her daughter was living through. Sarah

Grace had always been so tenderhearted, so trusting. Perhaps she'd been *too* trusting.

And then came Josh the Jerk, as Ellen now called him.

Once, he went to Washington, DC, for a conference, and while there, he bought Ellen a teacup at the Smithsonian. It was a nice Russian teacup with a floral design, but Josh apparently hadn't noticed that she collected only vintage English teacups with roses on them. For Sarah Grace's sake, Ellen displayed the teacup in the dining room with all the others, but the gaudy colors stuck out like a sore thumb.

As Ellen turned the situation over in her mind that morning, she walked into the dining room, picked up that Russian cup and saucer, and decided to have a little fun. First, she found some old T.J. Maxx bags under a kitchen cabinet and rather unceremoniously dropped the cup and saucer inside one. *Oops. Is that the sound of china banging together? Too bad!*

She walked out to the garage, home of Ed's tools and her own pink-handled tool set. She opened the case. Good. Ed hadn't swiped her hammer this time.

Ellen didn't want any of the neighbors watching what she was about to do, so she walked around back to the patio. The concrete patio.

And oops again—*What a klutz I am this morning!*—she dropped the bag containing the teacup and saucer right onto the concrete.

Gripping her hammer, Ellen bent over and started beating the daylights out of that teacup. She didn't normally have a violent nature, or at least she didn't think she did, yet she wielded that hammer like a crazy woman. And she enjoyed every minute of it.

A hammer, it turned out, was a dandy tool for smashing teacups.

"This," she said, quietly and firmly, "is for breaking up with my little girl."

Wham.

"And this," she said, "is for doing it in a lousy text message!"

Wham!

"And THIS," she said, "is just because I never liked you anyway, loser!"

WHAM!

She hammered the teacup again and again, stopping only when the bag split and shards of china began to spill out. Ellen briefly had the thought that she could use them for a mosaic project, but she decided she didn't want anything that reminded her of Josh in the house and took them to the trash can in the garage.

That afternoon, Sarah Grace dropped by to report on her day at school. She entered through the garage, and Ellen had to compose her face when her daughter held up a shard of china and asked if it came from the teacup Josh had given her.

"Yes," Ellen said. "It got broken, and I had to throw it away."

"Oh." Sarah Grace fingered the remnant of the teacup and tossed it in the kitchen trash. "Good. I'm *glad* it got broken."

Ellen relaxed for the first time all day. "Me too, honey. Me too."

7
A Friendly Valentine

*E*lizabeth Pinson's third graders couldn't wait for their Valentine's Day party to begin on that Thursday in 1952.

The children had been preparing for more than a week. They'd colored dozens of hearts and paper lace doilies to adorn the walls. Most of the hearts were pink and red, but Timmy Wilson colored his green. Timmy never did like to play by the rules.

Room mothers had dropped by all week, asking Miss Pinson if she needed help with the party and whether she had enough treats promised.

As always, there would be plenty with enough left over to feed another classroom or two. So far, the mothers were bringing iced sugar cookies, brownies, potato chips, peanuts, pimiento cheese finger sandwiches, and a sheet cake from

Butterfield's Grocery Store. Lucy Butterfield was in the class this year, and Mrs. Butterfield donated fancy sheet cakes from her husband's store at every opportunity.

On Wednesday, the children had decorated paper bags to hold their Valentines. While Miss Pinson usually tried to see that the bags looked similar, this year she let the children decorate the bags however they liked. She'd read an article about the importance of letting students show their individuality.

The girls drew hearts and flowers on theirs, and some of the boys took the liberty of drawing their favorite cartoon characters, including Howdy Doody and Joe Palooka.

Miss Pinson hoped the day would be fun, but mostly she hoped that the handsome new P.E. teacher, Walter Elliott, would pay her a visit. He'd been dropping by a lot lately to deliver messages from the office or ask her opinion about a student. Was it just her imagination or was Walter angling for a date? At twenty-three, Miss Pinson was starting to feel like a spinster. Secretly, she hoped for a little male attention this Valentine's Day.

The children had placed Valentine cards in their paper bags first thing that morning. After lunch, it was time to open them all. There were loads of Valentines. Miss Pinson always purchased extras to make sure no child was left out. Some, she signed "Your Secret Admirer" or "Guess who?" The children always loved thinking they had a secret admirer. A few boys said "Yuck!" when they opened those cards, but then Miss Pinson would see them looking around the classroom as if trying to guess the identity of the secret admirer.

The hour for the party arrived, and the treats poured in. The Butterfield sheet cake was a pink and red masterpiece. Thick strands of red icing spelled "Happy Valentine's Day," and pink shell-shaped icing trimmed the borders of the cake. Miss Pinson was glad the party was held near the end of the school day. These children would be buzzing with sugar before the afternoon was over.

She planned to take a piece of cake home with her for her afternoon teatime. Miss Pinson loved tea, something all the children knew about her. She even kept a pretty pink teacup on her desk. It held the stray pencil erasers and marbles she often picked up after class.

As room mothers hovered near the food table, there was a knock at the door. Miss Pinson asked Timmy to answer it.

"It's Mr. Elliott," he said.

She walked over to the door.

"Hi, Walter," she said, lowering her voice so the children wouldn't hear her addressing him by his first name.

"Hi, Elizabeth," he said. "Listen, uh, well ... here." He thrust a heart-shaped pink satin box at her. "I heard you tell one of the other teachers that you like chocolate and, well, I wanted you to have some."

"That's thoughtful of you, Walter," she said.

"And ..."

"Yes?"

"I was wondering ... would you like to have dinner with me tomorrow night?"

"I'd love to," she said, smiling. A tug at her skirt from Timmy brought her back to reality. He nodded at the tall woman beside him.

"Miss Pinson, the children want you to open your gift from the class now," said one of the room mothers volunteering at the party.

"Of course. I'll be right there," she said.

"Listen, thanks, Walter. And—"

"I know. You've got to get back," he said. "I'll pick you up at seven tomorrow night, okay?"

"Okay," she said. "I'll look forward to it."

In the classroom, the room mothers whispered. Miss Pinson could tell they were eager to watch her open a special gift from the class.

"I know what it is," teased Lucy Butterfield.

"Well, I don't," Miss Pinson said, grinning as she tore into the gaily wrapped package. She opened the box and pulled out a beautiful pink teapot that exactly matched the teacup on her desk. "I love it," she said, holding it up for the class to admire. She thanked everyone profusely before the mothers and students headed off, the party over.

Most of the students had gone home for the day when,

around three thirty, Timmy Wilson walked up to her desk.

"I forgot to give you this," he said, handing her a small white envelope and quickly scooting off.

"Thanks, Timmy," she called out, hoping he'd heard her.

She opened the envelope and pulled out one of the loveliest Valentines she had ever received. It showed a bouquet of flowers in a teacup with a heart on it. "A Friendly Valentine," it read. Inside it said simply, "Love, Timmy."

She had received a surprise box of chocolates from Walter and now a surprise Valentine from Timmy. Miss Pinson couldn't help thinking that Cupid had been very, very good to her that year.

With a small slice of Butterfield sheet cake wrapped in foil and tucked carefully in her pocketbook, Miss Pinson turned out the classroom light and headed home.

It was almost time for tea.

8
A Taste of Wisdom

Susan and Marleen had two o'clock reservations at the Wisdom Tea House, the new tearoom downtown. Susan was eager to try it out, but Marleen wasn't so sure. This tearoom offered a "contemporary" tea experience, and Marleen feared it would be one of those hippie tearooms she'd read about, one where middle-aged ladies wearing crystals and Birkenstocks came to plan their peace rallies.

Marleen vastly preferred the English afternoon tea experience. She liked seeing English bone china and perhaps some doilies on the table and vintage hats on the wall. Susan, however, was weary of those pink-and-chintz tearooms and eager to try something new.

The moment they entered Wisdom Tea House, Susan's eyes lit up. Finally! Susan loved drinking tea, especially Japanese greens, but she wasn't into the little-old-ladies-and-white-gloves mind-set. This tearoom seemed designed for modern sensibilities.

As they were seated, Marleen tried to conceal her disappointment. Everything was so simple and stark, with plain white cups and saucers before them, no rose-patterned china in sight.

A young woman in black slacks and a white blouse approached to take their tea order. Marleen tried not to be distracted by the blue streak in their server's jet-black hair. Caitlyn was the young woman's name, and Susan asked Caitlyn which green teas she recommended.

"Are you familiar with Japanese greens?" Caitlyn asked.

"They're my favorite," said Susan. "I like most senchas."

"In that case," Caitlyn said, "I'd recommend the Organic Sencha. We got in a new shipment yesterday, so it's quite fresh."

"Perfect," said Susan.

"And you, ma'am?" Caitlyn asked Marleen.

"I'll have the English Rose tea," she replied.

"Good choice," said Caitlyn, surprising her. "Some people find the rose taste too perfumey, but I've always loved it myself." With a nod of her head, she was off, and Susan and Marleen studied the rectangular ivory menus featuring a graphic of two leaves and a bud.

"I'm ordering the full afternoon tea," said Susan. "What about you?"

"Why not?" said Marleen, trying to get into the spirit of the place. The server had encouraged her by actually liking the rose-flavored tea.

When their tea arrived, Marleen noticed that Caitlyn placed each small brown earthenware teapot onto a beautifully quilted and padded fabric square.

"How lovely," she said. Marleen had quilted for years, and needlework always caught her eye.

"Aren't these great?" Caitlyn said. "The owner's mother makes them just for us, both to use and to sell in the gift shop. There's some sort of special fabric on the bottom that keeps hot teapots from scorching the tables. We had so many requests, she started making them for us to sell. She splits the proceeds between her church's food pantry and a girls' school in India. It's located near Darjeeling, and the owner learned about it at a tea conference."

Marleen was impressed.

Soon the first course appeared, and the two friends couldn't wait to start enjoying it.

"Our quiche today is a vegetarian asparagus quiche. If you need any refills on your tea, just let me know," Caitlyn said.

Both women still had plenty of tea, so they tucked into their quiche slices with great gusto.

"This is divine," said Marleen.

"Mmm, I agree," Susan mumbled between bites. "I was starving!"

Next came a black wrought-iron stand containing their savories, scones, and sweets. There was a beautiful array of foods that included turkey and arugula finger sandwiches, curry chicken salad bites rolled in almonds, plain and hazelnut scones, and scrumptious dessert offerings that had them both drooling.

Susan reached for a sandwich, and Marleen sat admiring it all.

"This is pretty tasty," said Susan, nodding at the egg salad sandwich in her hand. "Eat up!"

By the time they'd polished off the last scone, Marleen was stuffed. She ate a bite of an apricot square and half a white chocolate truffle before announcing she was done. Caitlyn brought her a box for the leftovers.

After seeing a poster about the tearoom's upcoming tea tasting, Susan headed to the office to make her reservation while Marleen browsed through baskets of quilted hotpads. Susan quietly handed the owner a twenty-dollar bill and said, "This is for your mother's church food pantry. Please tell her I admire what she's doing."

In the gift shop, Marleen looked around to make sure Susan couldn't see her handing over a check and hear her telling Caitlyn, "Please add this to the fund for those girls in India. I love that you support education in this way."

Marleen pondered the fact she'd been quite wrong about this "hippie" tearoom. She was so glad they'd come.

As they left the Wisdom Tea House, a young college student wearing a Grateful Dead T-shirt and jeans entered, her ragged gray backpack hanging off one arm. She glanced at Marleen's decorative pink jacket with teapot appliques on it. *Just the sort of woman I expected to find here,* she thought.

The young woman requested a table and sat down before unzipping her backpack, pulling out her laptop, and opening it.

She typed, "As a sociology class assignment, I am sitting here in a tearoom watching a bunch of middle-aged ladies have tea and crumpets. I doubt they'll have much that's good to eat here, so I texted Dave and told him I'd meet him for sushi in an hour. Hope I can survive that long."

"Hi. I'm Caitlyn. Do you know what kind of tea you'd like, or would you prefer to see a menu?"

"I usually drink oolongs," said the young woman, fully expecting the tea choices to be Tetley and Lipton.

"Terrific," said Caitlyn, pointing to the back of the tea menu. "Here are the oolongs, and our latest order included some Taiwanese oolongs that are excellent. Let me know if I can help you select one. I'll be back in a few minutes."

They serve oolongs here? thought the young woman. *Maybe this place won't be so bad after all …*

A Year of Teatime Tales

9
The Silverdale Dishes

Mornings start early up here in the North Georgia mountains. I usually get up when Lloyd does, around five or five thirty most days. I like to have my first cup of tea while it's still dark outside and quiet inside.

My husband is a hard worker and a good provider for our family. Things are rough for so many people these days, I can't complain. We made it through 1934, and I just know the good Lord is going to see us through 1935 too.

This morning, Lloyd and I are going into town to pick up our spring seed order at Wilson's Feed and Seed. Sure hope we have a good crop this spring and summer. I plan to can even more than I did last year. With three big, strapping boys, I can hardly cook enough to keep them full these days. The two girls just pick at their food, but that's a girl for you. The boys, though, I'll swanee, I can hardly cook it fast enough for them.

Yesterday at breakfast, I thought Zeb and Eddie and Richard were going to fight over that last biscuit. Those three worry me. They love to read about the war and all the things that happened in Europe not so long ago. Zeb says he'd love to go overseas and fight for this country. I'm just glad my boys are too young to be involved in anything like that. I hope there won't ever be another war.

While Lloyd and I are gone to town, Myrtle and Louise will give a good cleaning to the kitchen. The cabinets smell like bacon grease, and I don't like that one bit. Besides, we ought to tidy up some since I'm about to bring some nice new dishes into this house.

Lloyd and I have never been what you might call fancy people. We're just plain folks. But I do like for things to look nice. I like for my pound cakes to turn out pretty, and I like my biscuits to be nice and uniform, cut out perfectly round with the biscuit cutter. Thanks to Lloyd—and the chickens, of course—my kitchen's about to look even nicer, because I'm headed to pick up the prettiest set of blue dishes I've ever laid eyes on.

Wilson's Feed and Seed is next to Alley Brothers Dry Goods, and on trips to town, I always go in Alley's to pick up provisions. Sometimes it's a bag of flour, sometimes it's buttons, or maybe it's some thread if I've been patching up the boys' jeans. One day, I was in Alley's when a salesman stopped by with these beautiful blue dishes. The pattern was called "Silverdale," and it was made by a company called Swinnertons way over in London, England. "Silverdale" is such a pretty name.

I told that salesman I had no need for pretty dishes like that here on the farm. Why, the boys would bang them up in no time, and there I'd be, with a bunch of chipped and cracked dishes on my hands. At least, that's what I told Lloyd when we left the store that day.

When we got home, Lloyd said, "Helen, you've been talking 'bout them dishes all morning. You liked 'em, didn't ya?" I hadn't even realized I'd been going on about them. Goodness knows I didn't want Lloyd thinking I was hankering for a set of dishes, of all crazy things. Times are hard enough without us wasting hard-earned money on anything that isn't a necessity.

"No, Lloyd. They were pretty is all. But I have no need for such as that." I remember that Lloyd just nodded. And that, I thought, was that.

The next time Lloyd went into town, he came back with a sales ticket from Alley Brothers Dry Goods. "Here," he said, handing me the ticket.

"What's this?"

"I just paid down on those Silverdale dishes for you. I want you to take that egg money you always save for a rainy day and use it for those dishes. Our money situation's improved some, and I don't see why my wife can't have a nice set of dishes."

I nearly fell over dead. I wanted to ask him who he was and what he'd done with Lloyd. Instead, I just said, "Why, thank you, Lloyd."

That was six months ago. Little by little, I've been watching that egg money grow. Neighbors who don't have chickens have bought my eggs for years, and I've saved a tidy little sum thanks to those eggs. Now, every time those chickens lay an egg, I could just about kiss 'em, just thinking about how pretty those new dishes will look in my kitchen.

The boys, by the way, won't be using them. Lloyd and I agree on that. I'll use them when my sisters stop by for a cup of tea or coffee, or when the preacher's wife comes in for a visit. I might even sew up some napkins and get the girls to embroider daisies on them.

The old grandfather clock in the corner shows that it's nearly nine o'clock now, and I can't believe I'm soon going to be drinking my morning cup of tea out of a brand new cup that came all the way across the ocean from London, England. I've tried not to act too excited about it, even though it's not every day something so nice comes into this house.

"Helen, you ready to head into town in a bit?" Lloyd calls from the porch. He's been giving the boys their chores for the day.

I wipe down the kitchen counter and set my old, stained ironstone cup upside down on the draining rack.

"Yes, Lloyd, I'm ready," I say.

After drying my hands on the dish towel, I untie my apron, gather my pocketbook, and reach for my old blue hat. It's time to bring my new dishes home.

10
On Kindness and Carrots

You never forget your first love, and that applies to more than just romance. Decades have passed, yet I still remember when I first fell in love with teatime. And I can recall the taste of that tearoom's incredible soup as if I'd eaten it only yesterday.

My friend Kimberly and I, students at the University of Arkansas, were back home in Bentonville that weekend for Kimberly's birthday. My mother, eager to encourage anything ladylike, was treating the two of us to tea as Kimberly's birthday gift. She'd made reservations at the Victorian Village

Tearoom in Eureka Springs, a beautiful Ozark Mountain town beloved by tourists and locals alike. Kimberly and I adored everything Victorian, and I was excited to be going to tea.

That Saturday was sunny, and I remember that Whitney Houston's upbeat "I Wanna Dance With Somebody" was blaring from my Ford Tempo's cassette tape player when I picked up Kimberly. I wore my new Laura Ashley cabbage rose dress with a Battenburg lace collar. Kimberly wore an ivory lace blouse and a ruffled pink skirt with a matching eel skin belt. I also remember that she'd gotten a gift of some new gold beads for her Add-A-Bead necklace, which was almost full. Next to hers, mine looked like a Sad-A-Bead necklace.

On the way to Eureka Springs, we discussed what teatime might be like. Mom had said to be sure and keep my pinkie extended as I sipped tea, as that was the proper thing to do—and I had a hard time being proper. I loved the Victorian period, but I was also a tomboy who played basketball and tennis. Kimberly was the girly one, not me.

Upon arriving at the tearoom, we saw they had written our names on a blackboard out front. "Welcome, Kimberly and Jennifer. Happy Birthday, Kimberly!"

A friendly brunette greeted us and said we'd be dining in the Victorian Parlor. We were promptly ushered into a high-ceilinged room and seated on a mahogany sofa upholstered in burgundy velvet. A marble-topped table sat before us, already set with floral teacups and napkins.

The waitress gave us a list of five teas to select from. Kimberly chose Earl Grey, and I chose English Afternoon Tea because I liked anything English. After our tea was poured, I was surprised to find how much I enjoyed hot tea. Growing up in the South, I drank lots of iced tea but never hot tea. At school, I lived on Diet Coke.

A mother and daughter came into the parlor and were seated at a small table in the corner. The little girl whispered to her mother and pointed at Kimberly. I assumed she was admiring Kimberly's gorgeous hair. She'd just gotten a new spiral perm, and her amazing golden halo ensured she never lacked for a boyfriend—or admirers in general. I, however, still sported the short hair and feathery bangs I'd gotten in my well-intended if unsuccessful attempt to look like Princess Di.

The waitress said our tea tray was almost ready, and while we waited, she offered us a cup of their famous Carrot Soup, served in another elegant teacup. Carrot Soup didn't sound so great to me, but Kimberly and I had manners enough to take a cup and give it a try.

"You go first," I said.

She did. "Oh, wow!"

"Wow-good or wow-bad?"

"Take a bite."

I spooned past some froufrou "roses" made of carrot curls and tasted the richest, creamiest, most velvety goodness I had ever eaten.

"This can't be carrots," I said. "Tastes way too good." I normally lived off Pringles potato chips, Snickers bars, and Taco Bell burritos, so if I liked the stuff, that was saying something. I asked the waitress what was in the soup besides carrots. She smiled politely and said it was a secret family recipe, but she'd be glad to have the owner send some soup home with us. Thinking of my empty dorm room refrigerator, I accepted the offer.

As we attacked the tea tray, Kimberly and I giggled like schoolgirls and spoke with fake British accents. There we were, college students, dining like the Queen with this fancy metal stand that had three different plates of food on it. There were tea sandwiches, scones, tiny desserts—even chocolate-covered strawberries.

Kimberly loved sweets and went straight for the top plate, quickly devouring her strawberry, brownie bite, lemon square, and a fruit tart thingie. I ate five sandwiches, which were so good, and had a scone and some sweets as well.

When we finished, the waitress told us we were welcome to look around the rest of the tearoom, and we did. The rooms were so elegant with their ruffled curtains and artwork of Victorian ladies. Kimberly said her mom, an antiques dealer, would love their decor.

When it was time to leave and I asked about leaving the tip, the waitress told us that, too, had been taken care of in advance by my mom—which didn't surprise me. What did surprise me was that the tearoom owner had heard how much we enjoyed her Carrot Soup and brought us a white plastic bag containing two huge Styrofoam containers of it, lids on top and tightly wrapped.

Kimberly suggested I hang on to the soup, and after we both got back to campus Sunday night, she'd come to my room and we'd eat.

When Sunday night rolled around, Kimberly came over and, when we got hungry, pulled the crinkled bag out of my mini fridge.

She opened the bag, removed the containers, and with a puzzled look, pulled out a white index card.

"What's that?" I said.

"It's the recipe for this Carrot Soup!"

I remember that act of kindness to two college girls to this day. And when I say I can still remember that soup as though I ate it yesterday, that's because ... I did.

A Year of Teatime Tales

11
The Legend of the Shamrock Teacup

Once upon a time, in the beautiful Irish countryside, there lived a handsome leprechaun named Liam. He was constantly leading friends into mischief, but he was a well-loved leprechaun nonetheless.

One year as St. Patrick's Day approached, Liam rounded up some pals and said he wanted to celebrate the holiday out of the country for a change.

"Where?" said his friend Loughlin.

"Why?" said his friend Leary.

"My friends, we're going to England to seek an adventure," Liam replied.

"England?" said Leary. "They probably don't even know how to celebrate the day over there."

"They most certainly do!" said Liam. "Just pack your bags and meet me at the airport in Dublin in an hour."

Leprechauns could time travel and did not, in fact, have to fly, but Liam and his friends could make themselves invisible and liked to hitchhike in a plane's cargo hold, so that was how they traveled to England.

Upon their arrival at Heathrow, Liam boarded a shuttle and told his friends to follow him.

"Where are we going now?" asked Loughlin, who was always up for a good time.

"I still don't see why we have to make this bloody trip," said Leary, his disposition as sunny as always.

"You'll see," said Liam.

Soon, they left the hustle and bustle of London behind, and the landscape turned to rolling hillsides and farmland. They approached a sign reading "Stoke-on-Trent," and Liam pointed, announcing, "That's where we're going, my friends!"

"Oh boy!" said Loughlin.

"Whatever for?" said Leary.

"You'll see," said Liam.

The leprechauns checked into their room at the Royal Crown Inn and Pub in Stoke-on-Trent. Leprechaun check-in was quite a different matter than check-in for humans. For the leprechaun, it simply meant running up and down the halls of the inn, spying out the very best room, and waiting until the occupants left. The leprechauns then stretched themselves out flatter than a crumpet and slid under the door.

"Friends," Liam said once they had settled in, "I can now tell you why we're here. We're going to tour the potteries!"

"Hurray!" said Loughlin.

"Potteries? Why would we want to go there?" grumbled Leary.

"You'll see," said Liam.

Some American tourists staying at the inn had arranged to visit the potteries too. When Liam overheard the ladies talking, he and his friends decided to hop in the backseat of their SUV, in the tiny spots next to the pocketbooks, and hitch a ride.

Once they arrived at the potteries, Liam was first to leap out of the car. "Follow me!" he said.

Inside the first factory they toured, Liam and his friends peered around, wide-eyed, at the vast array of kilns and the teawares that had been produced there. Liam was quite the fan of Irish Breakfast tea and appreciated a good teacup.

"So this is where it all begins!" said Loughlin, impressed.

"Humph," said Leary.

"This way," said Liam. "But first, I have to ask you fellows a question. St. Patrick's Day is coming up, and I have a rather incredible idea for making sure this is one we'll never forget. Are you in?"

"I'm in," said Loughlin.

"What choice do I have?" said Leary.

"Good," said Liam. "Come with me."

They entered a room where workers applied transfers to new china wares. Floral designs were the favorites in that room. Liam overheard a woman named Cathleen say they were busy filling the orders of Americans who wanted festive new teawares in time for St. Patrick's Day.

"I've always loved St. Patrick," Cathleen told her coworker Gail. "You know what great symbol is associated with St. Patrick, don't you?"

"Can't say as I do," said Gail, looking at her watch. She was ticking off the minutes until the next smoke break.

"It's a wonderful bit of symbolism," said Cathleen. "When St. Patrick was helping spread Christianity all over Ireland, it occurred to him he had the perfect symbol for the trinity right there in his own backyard."

"And what might that have been?" said the coworker, slightly interested.

"Why, the shamrock, of course!" said Cathleen. "Just as the clover is made up of three leaves, so the Holy Trinity consists of Father, Son, and Holy Spirit, three in one. Quite lovely."

"How 'bout that," said Gail, who thought that religious folk could be a pain in the bum sometimes.

"It's a pity we've run out of shamrocks this year," Cathleen said. "The manager says we could have all gotten a nice bonus if we just had a few more shamrock teacups to send to America."

Just then, Liam told his friends of his extraordinary plan.

"Here's the deal. You know how we flattened ourselves out a few hours ago and snuck under the door of our room at the inn?"

The friends nodded.

"I say, let's flatten ourselves out into small shamrock shapes, quietly attach ourselves to some teacups, and we'll get a free trip to America! We'll have to stick close to the teacups each March, but the other eleven months we'll be free to explore and have a grand time. Why, we can even go back home to Ireland most of the year if we like!"

"What a great plan!" said Loughlin.

"That's the dumbest thing I've ever heard," said Leary. "But don't leave me behind!"

And so it was that while the pottery workers went on break one day, Liam and his friends disguised themselves as shamrocks and climbed onto a teacup, which a darling woman named Cathleen was absolutely delighted to find and ship off to the States.

So in America, very early on the morning of every March 17, Liam and his friends departed their teacup home and ran to their nearest Mass to pray and remember St. Patrick, dashing back well before the homeowner had risen.

That was just an old legend, though, for leprechauns couldn't turn themselves into shamrocks. Could they?

12
A Growing Friendship

After enduring such a cold and wet winter, Joanne was ready to play in the dirt again. The first day of spring was one she always looked forward to, and this year she was especially eager for it. Her husband, Tom, had promised to build her a new garden shed. The two of them were in their seventies now and still enjoyed good health, so she saw no reason not to plan for the future as if she would have one.

Joanne had owned garden sheds of every shape, size, and color for thirty years now, but this time she wanted a small white cottage near the edge of the woods. Tom had been collecting all the old doors and windows he could find to make it happen. He was waiting for the ground to dry out a bit before he started on the foundation, but he'd given Joanne the go-ahead to start getting plants and decor ready.

In the garage, Joanne found the usual pile of garden pots and statuary that she always tossed inside at the last minute each fall. Typically, she waited for news of a freeze and rushed outdoors to collect any objects that might break. She'd learned the hard way that birdfeeders made of glass looked pretty during warm weather, but after they'd filled with water, frozen, and shattered—not so much.

The all-white garden cottage had been the focus of her reading and planning all winter. She kept a notebook where she taped photos from garden magazines and listed names of plants she wanted to grow. Joanne could hardly wait to watch it all come to life. Spring was definitely the season for the world's dreamers and optimists.

Daffodils had been popping up in the neighborhood lawns for weeks, and in her cottage garden out front, the frilly burgundy foliage of the peonies was just coming up. Of course, the weeds were in abundance as well. Tom called those the zombies of the plant world, noting that you could try to get rid of them, but they were indestructible and never really died.

Clay pots. That was what Joanne needed, her clay pots.

She loved seeing all the colorful ceramic pots in the garden center each spring, but when it got down to the serious business of potting and repotting plants, she found nothing did the job quite as well as a plain old clay pot.

She pulled out a box from beneath a shelf in the garage and found a dozen or so. Good. She already knew what she was going to plant around the new garden shed this year. She would have lemon basil, French thyme, cilantro, and several varieties of mint—the mint in pots because it was so invasive and would overtake her lawn if she didn't corral it from the get-go.

Next, Joanne pulled out the box with her decorative garden pieces. The small mosaic fountain was a favorite and always created such a bright spot in the garden. The wire teapot planter had been a gift from one of her Red Hat

Society friends a few Christmases ago. It had arrived with a poinsettia in it, and Joanne had often mourned the fact that poinsettias couldn't grow outside year-round.

She still hadn't found the planter she was looking for. It had been a gift from her gardener friend Marian, and it was perhaps the most treasured pot she had. Marian had died of a heart attack two years ago, and Joanne still felt the loss deeply. The two had been close friends, talking on the phone almost every day, getting together for lunch every Wednesday, and constantly seeing each other at church. And then, just like that, Marian was gone.

The two of them had talked on the phone the very morning Marian passed away, making it all the more difficult for Joanne to accept when Marian's daughter called with the devastating news. Marian had been out separating the Siberian irises, and her daughter took comfort in the fact that at least her mother got to spend her last hours on earth doing what she enjoyed most—tending her garden.

Joanne hoped she would be so lucky as to take her last breaths outdoors while enjoying the beauty of nature.

Finally, Joanne spotted the earth-toned teacup planter in a box with some gardening tools she'd tucked away. She took the planter inside the house, rinsed off the dust and cobwebs, and carried it outside to the potting bench that she was using until the new garden shed made its debut.

There sat a small black plastic pot, and in it was a plant with lots of silvery-green foliage and tiny violet-blue blossoms. The plant was one she'd grown with seeds from Marian, who insisted on calling her plants by the Latin name. That one was 'Myosotis sylvatica.'

Joanne removed the plant from its plastic pot, poured some potting soil into the teacup planter, and brushed away the excess soil before nestling the young plant inside. "There," she said, pleased with her work. "For you, Marian."

When the little white cottage was complete and it was time to settle in, Joanne would invite a few friends over to celebrate. Marian would have been so excited about the new garden shed, and Joanne wanted her to somehow be a part of it.

Now—thanks quite literally to the seeds she'd sown—Marian's garden legacy would live on. For while Marian had preferred to call plants by the Latin name, Joanne did not. She intended to tell any visitor who asked that the sweet violet-blue blossoms in the teacup planter came from an old friend—and they were called Forget-me-nots.

A Year of Teatime Tales

13
The Rhinestone Teapot Pin

We all had that one friend who made us wonder why on earth we kept them around. Mine was Judy.

That morning, Judy and I were out junkin', hitting the local estate sales. We'd been junkin' buddies for years, and each of us knew exactly what the other was looking for. One of the best estate sales on my list was about thirty minutes away, so I picked up Judy at seven a.m. sharp.

Judy's problem was that she didn't have a filter. She never thought about whether or not it was appropriate to say something. If the woman thought it, she said it. Period.

Judy's kids gave her a Kindle Fire for her birthday last week, and now she wouldn't go anywhere without it. Judy had never been on social media before, and her kids signed her up on Facebook. I could have killed them.

Before I'd even finished my travel mug of English Breakfast tea, Judy said, "Did you know that during the Middle Ages, they treated hemorrhoids with hot irons? What they would do is—"

"I don't want to hear about hemorrhoids from the Middle Ages this early in the morning," I said. Actually, I didn't want to hear about them anytime.

"Bill has hemorrhoids real bad, and he—"

"Oversharing."

"Dang, Elizabeth. Why are you so grumpy?"

"I'm not. I'm trying to wake up."

"Fine."

We rode in silence for a blessed fifteen seconds before she was at it again, scrolling through Facebook on her Kindle and laughing. I wasn't about to ask what she found so funny.

"These dancing orangutans are cracking me up," she said.

"Uh-huh," I said, not taking my eyes off the road.

"No, seriously. Look at this video." Judy shoved her Kindle on top of my steering wheel.

"Hey, I can't watch that and drive at the same time."

"You're no fun," she said.

A few minutes later, she moved on to another topic. "Did you know Mary Jenkins isn't speaking to Lisa? It's all over Facebook. She got mad because—"

"Say, did you bring that list of pieces you're looking for in your Depression glass pattern?"

Judy collected Buttons and Bows Depression glass—the pink but not the iridescent—and was always looking for new pieces. If I could distract her with that, maybe she would quit obsessing over random posts on Facebook.

To my amazement, she turned off the Kindle and reached into her pocketbook for a small notepad.

"Got it right here," she said. "I need three more dinner plates, one cup and saucer, two sherbet dishes, and the oval vegetable bowl. Then I'll have service for eight, and that's all I want for now."

"I'm not really looking for anything special today," I said. "Just my same old list—teapots, teacups, pretty silverplate, and old cookbooks."

"The usual?" she said.

I nodded. I spotted a sign for the estate sale, turned

down a side street, and parked a few minutes later. Only a few cars were there, but it was time to go ahead and claim our numbers. The folks who ran the estate sale always gave us a number in the order in which we arrived, and then at opening, they let us enter a few at a time.

We were numbers eight and nine in line, so we'd likely be part of the first group to enter. At eight on the dot, they waved us inside. I glanced at the living room and walked past, headed for the kitchen. Judy did, too, because that was where we usually found Depression glass and teawares. I saw a counter stacked with pink glassware and hoped Judy would find some items she wanted.

The open cabinet doors revealed a display of teapots. I was excited to see a pink Aladdin teapot, which had long been on my wish list. It looked great. I ran a finger around the lid, spout, and base but couldn't feel any chips or cracks. The teapot was marked eight dollars, so it was definitely going home with me.

Surprisingly, Judy and I were the only ones in the kitchen.

"Any Buttons and Bows?" I asked.

"Just nabbed this vegetable bowl and two sherbets," she said, holding up the pieces in triumph.

"Excellent."

Judy scanned the rest of the kitchen but apparently didn't find anything else she wanted. She said she was taking her glassware to the checkout table so the gals there could go ahead and box it. Then, she said that in the preview pictures online, she'd seen some old costume jewelry they had for sale, so she was going to check that out while I continued looking at vintage Pyrex dishes. Those small refrigerator dishes were quite fetching, and I'd been thinking of collecting them.

Within minutes, Judy returned and held out her hand. I was afraid she'd gotten out her Kindle and had something for me to view on Facebook. Instead, it was a rhinestone pin in the shape of a teapot.

"Thought you might like this," she said.

"It's adorable."

"Pins are just three dollars each."

"Thanks," I said. "I love it. Listen, give me another minute to check out the Pyrex, and I'll be up to pay. I want to hit a couple of other sales before the crowds get there this morning."

When I got to the cashier, I saw Judy had whipped out her Kindle. "Did you know that during the Middle Ages—"

"Hey!" I said, a little too loudly. "Just wanted you to know I'm here and ready to pay." To the cashier I said, "Look what my friend found for me."

Judy beamed like a proud mother.

"I knew someone would want that old teapot pin," the cashier said. "I'm glad it's going to a good home."

And it was. The pin was a little loud for my tastes, a little gaudy, and a little tarnished—kind of like Judy, now that I thought about it. But I decided I'd keep them both.

A Year of Teatime Tales

🕮 14 🕮
A Cup of Easter Tea

Joanna had always loved going to church on Easter Sunday. She enjoyed seeing the little girls in their frilly dresses, Easter hats, and white patent leather shoes. She loved seeing the little boys looking cute but uncomfortable in their Easter suits and ties. She loved seeing women wear their pretty new Easter dresses, some of them with matching hats, and she loved hearing the choir's soul-stirring hymns like "Christ the Lord is Risen Today."

The highlight of the Easter service was always the sermon, in which the pastor inevitably talked about how God loved the world so much, he sent his son Jesus to die on the cross so that whoever accepted him could have the gift of eternal life.

No matter how many times Joanna heard that message, she found that kind of love impossible to fathom. Her twin girls, Lindsey and Lauren, had just turned thirty, and Joanna couldn't have imagined letting them die in place of someone else. As a mother, she had decided years ago that she would simply never be able to comprehend how God was able to sacrifice his only child. As a believer, she was immensely grateful that he had.

The girls, both of whom had gotten married last year, lived nearby but were celebrating Easter with their respective in-laws out of town. Joanna had been a single mom since her husband left them all when the girls were three, and for the first time since she became a mom, she was spending the holiday by herself. She had always imagined she would spend most all holidays with her children, but she told herself she needed to let that dream die. The girls were married now and had lives of their own.

She woke to a light rain on Easter morning, but she couldn't be sad, because after all, it was Easter.

Friends who had learned she would be alone had invited her to join them for Easter dinner, but she knew she would feel like a fifth wheel. They were thoughtful to invite her, and she was grateful for the offers, but she just wanted to go home after church and enjoy a quiet Easter afternoon.

She'd bought a small ham at the grocery store and prepared it and some asparagus on Saturday, so after church she enjoyed a light meal and sank into the sofa for a nice nap.

Midafternoon, Joanna decided to have a cup of Easter Tea. A friend who'd been to London recently had brought her back a tin of Fortnum and Mason's Easter Tea blend, a wonderful black tea with marigold and sunflower blossoms.

She prepared a cup of the tea and reached into the kitchen linen drawer for one of the hand-painted napkins she'd recently found at an antique mall.

Joanna hadn't paid much attention to the floral designs on the napkins when she purchased them, so she was surprised to realize the one she was using had pale pink dogwood blossoms on it. She had always loved the legend of the dogwood, which her mother had shared with her when she was a child. According to the legend, during the time of Jesus, the dogwood had become a giant tree with strong, firm wood. The wood was so sturdy, in fact, it was chosen as the wood for Jesus's cross.

The dogwood, however, was dismayed to find itself being used for such a horrid purpose. While hanging on the cross, Jesus sensed the dogwood's shame and said, "Because of your sorrow over my suffering, you'll never again grow large enough to be used as a cross. From today on, you'll be slender and twisted, and your blossoms will take the shape of this cross—two long and two short petals, and with a crown of thorns in the middle."

As she sipped her Easter Tea and studied the dogwood blossoms on her napkin, she thought about some verses the pastor had shared during the morning's sermon. He'd read from Luke 24. *"Now upon the first day of the week, very early in the morning, they came unto the sepulchre, bringing the spices which they had prepared, and certain others with them. And they found the stone rolled away from the sepulchre. And they entered in, and found not the body of the Lord Jesus. ... It was Mary Magdalene, and Joanna, and Mary the mother of James, and other women that were with them, which told these things unto the apostles."*

That revelation had just floored Joanna the first time she heard it.

Why wasn't John the first person to report back to the others? He was, after all, the one so many thought was the "beloved" disciple. And she could certainly have understood if the first person to discover the empty tomb had been Peter, the guilt-ridden disciple who had denied Jesus three times. If there was anyone who had wanted to see Jesus alive and clear his conscience, it would have been Peter.

But a group of women? Why had they been given that special honor of telling the good news? She had to admit she was especially interested because one of the women shared her name.

Joanna sipped her tea and wondered if she would get to meet Bible Joanna in Heaven one day and ask her about that first resurrection morning. Why not? Maybe they'd even get to have a cup of tea together.

Before she got much deeper in thought, her reverie was interrupted by the doorbell. Joanna stepped into the foyer, looked out the French doors, and was delighted to see Lindsey and Lauren and their husbands standing there.

"What a surprise!" she said as she welcomed them inside.

"Happy Easter, Mom!" the girls said.

"Happy Easter yourself!" Joanna said, laughing and hugging them all. And it was, truly, one of the happiest Easters Joanna could remember, a day of good news from beginning to end—and forever.

15
Taking Tea with the Methodists

"Brenda Johnson, I cannot believe you have started going to the Methodists. What would your grandmama—God rest her soul—have thought about her only grandchild prancing off across town and leaving the Baptists without a decent organist on Sunday mornings? And to beat all, the Methodists have already got a good organist."

I couldn't believe what I was hearing through my cell phone. I thought this woman was my friend. "As I have tried to tell you, Mary Lou, this is something I felt like the Lord wanted me to do. If you have a problem with it, you need to take it up with HIM. And I'd appreciate it if you would not drag my sweet grandmama into this *personal* matter."

Mary Lou Carter and I had gone to church together ever since we were in the nursery, and she was having a hissy fit over the fact I'd decided to become a Methodist. She should have known I wouldn't have made such an important decision without a lot of prayer.

"I'm not buying that, not for one minute," Mary Lou said. "Everybody knows you got your feelings hurt when Starla Mooneyham didn't put your chicken salad biscuits on the menu for the Spring Tea and Luncheon."

"That is not true," I said. While Starla, who was in charge of the ladies ministry, had chosen other tea sandwiches, I *certainly* never expected that mine would automatically be selected—even if they *were* award-winning and the recipe was once printed in *Southern Lady* magazine. "And for your information, they are not *biscuits*. They are *croissants*. It's a French word, so I don't expect Baptists to be able to pronounce it, but—"

"So we're a bunch of bumpkins now that you're in with the Methodists. Is that it? We're not good enough anymore?"

Mary Lou sure had her knickers in a knot.

I sighed. "No, that's not it at all. I'm just saying that not everyone knows how to pronounce *croissants*, and they are not like biscuits. And to be honest with you, I had totally forgotten about y'all's little spring tea. That go off okay?"

"It wasn't the same without you there in charge of the tea service, but yeah, it went fine," Mary Lou said. "Starla's college roommate's sister-in-law was the speaker this year. She was all right, I guess, but some of the women said she spoke too long."

That didn't surprise me. I'd always kept my opinions about that sort of thing to myself, but Baptist luncheon speakers were not known for their brevity. Now the Methodists, those women knew how to book a good speaker.

"Glad to hear it went well," I said. "Listen, if you're not busy the first Saturday in May, you're welcome to come join us for our Mother's Day Tea."

"But you're not a mother, Brenda."

I got so tired of women pointing that out to me as if it was a news flash I had somehow missed for the past fifty-seven years.

"No, I'm not, but the Methodists believe in honoring *all* women, not just those who were blessed with children," I said. "Our assistant pastor, Emily Nelson, believes God gives some women physical children but all women have spiritual children."

Mary Lou's chuckle made me want to scream. "I forgot y'all have one of those lady preachers," she said.

I was not going into *that* with Mary Lou, that was for sure.

"So back to the Mother's Day Tea, I'd love for you to be my guest, especially since I'm on the program."

"Is that so? What are you gonna do?"

"I'm speaking on The Womanly Art of Hospitality," I said. "Several of the women knew about my being president of the Tea Society and asked if I'd speak."

"Sure, I'll come," Mary Lou said. "What do y'all eat? You don't have alcohol at Methodist tea parties, do you?"

I was starting to wish I hadn't asked Mary Lou to attend. "No, we don't have alcohol at our teas, or anything else at the church, for heaven's sake. This isn't the Country Club."

"Coulda fooled me," she muttered.

She really needed to let it go. I wished her and all my old church friends the best, really, I did, but it was clearly time for me to move on. I was not saying I'd outgrown them *spiritually*—that would be prideful, wouldn't it?—but again, as I told Mary Lou, I knew when the Lord was telling me I needed to become a Methodist.

I was trying to figure out how to end the call when Mary Lou asked the strangest question.

"So which of your tea sandwiches are you making for the tea?"

"How did you know I was making tea sandwiches?"

"Just a hunch," Mary Lou said. I could have sworn I heard her snicker.

"For your information, the Methodists don't have cliques like the Baptists, so anyone who wants to make tea sandwiches can volunteer and bring a tray. I'm making my Ham Salad Ladyfingers. These women are so appreciative too."

"I'm sure they are," said Mary Lou. "I hear half of 'em can't cook." That was rich coming from Mary Lou, whose only edible homemade food was pimiento cheese spread.

"There are some fine cooks at my new church," I said, "and I'm sure you'll agree once you see how *nice* a church tea can be."

Mary Lou had to go after that, and I'd never been so glad to say goodbye to a woman in my life. Besides, I needed to call the ladies in my new Bible study. They had asked me to be in charge of the refreshments each Tuesday morning.

I decided I'd go practice making some Ham Salad Ladyfingers while I thought about my speech for the Mother's Day Tea. It was so nice to be *appreciated*, unlike the way I was treated at my old church. I couldn't wait for Mary Lou to see what a wonderful time we would have at the tea!

16
She Dreams in Roses

Helen was out back tending to her irises when Malcolm walked up beside her.

"What are those things called again?" he said.

"Irises," she said. Malcolm was a lawn-mowing fiend when it came to keeping the grass cut, but he would never be mistaken for a Master Gardener. "And I just noticed some rosebuds, too, so hopefully we'll have roses soon."

"I saw where one of your pink roses bloomed out front this week."

"Where?"

"You know, over there with your rose bushes."

Helen walked briskly to the front of the house and looked at her David Austin English rose bushes. No buds. No blossoms.

Malcolm had followed her there. "It's that pink one"—he

pointed to a corner of the flower garden—"although it looks a little bent-over right now."

"That's a tulip, dear," she said, but she wasn't disappointed. Roses were welcome whenever they decided to arrive, and Helen didn't mind having to wait for something so lovely to appear.

As a gentle mist began to fall, she went inside the house to warm herself with a cup of tea and read her new issue of *Country Gardens* magazine. As she looked on the pantry shelf where she kept her tea tins, it occurred to her that she had been drinking more and more tea lately. Earl Grey and Lady Earl Grey. Darjeeling. Hot Cinnamon Spice. And there in the corner was a tea she'd forgotten about—a gold foil packet labeled Springtime Rose, a rose-flavored black tea she'd purchased at a tearoom a few months earlier.

Helen had recently invested in a teacup and saucer rack that hung in her kitchen. From it, she carefully removed a pretty bone china teacup with a salmon-pink rose on it. She fingered the cup while the stovetop kettle boiled the water.

The slow, leisurely ritual was one she never tired of. Helen measured a spoonful of tea into her stainless steel infuser basket, placed it in her teacup, and waited for the kettle to signal that her water was ready.

She fingered the cup and studied the rose. So simple. So lovely.

Helen had loved roses ever since she was a little girl, and she never forgot the woman who taught her to love them.

Grandma Mary lived out in the country in a rambling white two-story house with a wraparound porch that Helen remembered for its rocking chairs and the cousins who were usually filling them. The house was frequently a gathering place for her father's side of the family, and a visit to Grandma Mary's always meant Helen would get to visit with some cousin or other she didn't always get to see back in town.

Helen's grandmother loved her flower gardens, and Helen could never think of her grandmother without remembering her Mason jars and roses. Inevitably, the springtime porch would be perfumed with the scent of old-fashioned roses packed into Mason jars, spilling forth their sweet fragrance onto whichever family members happened to be visiting.

One spring when Helen was about six or so, her parents had to go out of town on business, and so she got to spend a week visiting her grandparents. That was back when Grandpa Harold was still alive. He'd been working the farm all day, so Helen helped her grandmother with the housekeeping and meal preparation. She could still taste the sausage from those hearty country breakfasts. Grandma Mary's sausage was legendary, and none Helen had tasted since had even come close to comparing to her grandmother's.

One day, the household chores were finished early. Lunch had been prepared and served, and the dishes had been cleared from the table and washed. Grandma Mary had dried her hands on her apron, taken Helen by the hand, and said, "Come on, sweetheart. Let's go visit my roses."

Grandma Mary had a special basket she liked to carry on her arm when she was tending to her roses. She would examine one blossom, then another, and eventually select one that she'd cut off with her pruning shears and place in the basket.

"See these thorns, child?" her grandmother had said. "Don't fear the thorns. They can hurt you only if you're not careful around them, and they're quite helpful to the roses. If there weren't any thorns, animals might eat the roses or climb up the bushes, and there we'd be—no beautiful roses for us to enjoy."

It was such a simple lesson, and Helen never forgot her grandmother's practical country wisdom.

Helen never forgot the scent of her grandmother's roses either. Grandma Mary liked deep red roses, and hers had those lush, velvety petals that smelled so sweet, the fragrance always lingered in the mind long after the rose itself had dropped its petals and withered away.

The whistle of the teakettle told Helen it was time to stop daydreaming and start steeping her cup of tea.

Malcolm walked by the kitchen and paused when he saw the teacup. "Now that's a rose and not a tulip," he said.

"That's correct, dear," Helen said.

Malcolm smiled and headed to the den.

Helen lingered over her teacup and inhaled deeply. A fragrance reminiscent of her grandmother's country roses wafted through the air.

And Helen realized it didn't matter at all whether she had roses blooming in her garden, for she would always have them blooming in her soul.

A Year of Teatime Tales

17
The Japanese Tea Set

Cathy loved to decorate, and while she wasn't into high-end design projects, she dearly loved to spruce up a room. In the kitchen, she would regularly hang new curtains over the kitchen sink. In the living room, she liked to switch out the pillows seasonally to bring new color into her decor. That big skirted table in her bedroom? It was forever being redecorated, sometimes with vintage books or, in summer, seashells collected on family beach trips.

But much as Cathy loved to decorate, in her dining room was one small vignette she'd been enjoying for months and never intended to change—ever.

To the casual visitor, it was simply a handsome oak cabinet displaying some vintage Japanese teawares in front of sepia-toned photos. Cathy usually favored a more streamlined look over a cluttered one, but every time she walked by the busy little tea scene, it gave her no small amount of pleasure to know these teawares were out where everyone could see and enjoy them.

The handpainted tea set featured a scene from a Japanese garden. The set had belonged to Cathy's great-grandmother and, through various handings-down in the family, eventually became hers. While her closest friends were quite familiar with the tea set, new friends would see the prettily faded photos behind the tea set and ask if that sweet little golden-haired child with the big bow in her hair was an ancestor. "Yes, that was my great-grandmother, and this tea set once belonged to her," Cathy would reply. And that was the truth. But it wasn't the whole truth.

The fact of the matter was, her great-grandmother—"Great-grandmother Lucille" as she insisted the great-grandchildren call her—was a stuffy old biddy. She wasn't a loving mother to Cathy's grandmother, she had never been very fond of Cathy's mother, and Cathy remembered her simply as the unpleasant old woman who spent the last years of her life terrorizing the rest of her family. She never played with her grandchildren and great-grandchildren—"too rambunctious," she always said—and family lore had it that she probably nagged her poor husband to an early death.

Cathy's mother once told her the real story behind Great-grandmother Lucille's tea set. When Lucille married Cathy's great-grandfather, a wealthy young banker named Harold, they'd gone on a tour of the Orient for their honeymoon. One of the many *objets d'art* Harold purchased for Lucille on that trip was a Japanese tea set that caught her fancy.

Was the tea set used with her husband or perhaps her children and grandchildren? No. Had it provided hospitality at women's club meetings and library fundraisers? No. Instead, Great-grandmother Lucille would pull out the tea set once a year to admire it, show off her priceless pieces of "art," and reminisce about her and Harold's honeymoon to any unfortunate relatives who happened to be within earshot. Then, she would wrap each of the pieces back in a soft cotton cloth and have the tea set returned to the attic for another year.

While Cathy never had great reason to dislike her great-grandmother, she didn't have warm feelings for her either, primarily because of the way the woman had treated her own daughter and granddaughter. Cathy often marveled that some of her friends went around pretending they had always had such perfect families when, in reality, everyone's family was usually dysfunctional in one way or another.

Years after Great-grandmother Lucille passed away, her tea set eventually got handed down to Cathy. She was determined those lovely old pieces were going to have a new life. She set them out in plain view on the oak cabinet in her dining room so that she and her family would see them every single day. She and her twelve-year-old daughter, Mallory, had already enjoyed a few impromptu teas using the tea set. If one of her teenage sons or their friends happened by one day and knocked a piece off, so be it, she said. What was that great old saying? "Love people, not things; use things, not people."

When Cathy inherited the tea set, she knew immediately that the revered pieces of "art" were going to have a new set of house rules. Cathy invited her mother over one Wednesday morning for brunch. They had a delicious quiche and some fresh fruit, and in the center of the table—right there in front of God and everybody—sat the infamous honeymoon souvenir that had spent a lifetime largely in hiding, Great-grandmother Lucille's Japanese Tea Set.

Her mom had stared at the set wide-eyed when she first realized Cathy was actually *using* the sacred tearwares. She never said a word about it, but Cathy suspected her mother was quietly pleased.

The photo of the smiling little blonde—the photo tucked behind a teapot on the old oak cabinet—had more than one story to tell. There was the story of a happy young child who grew up to be a very different sort of older woman. And then there was the story of the woman who overvalued her things. Cathy could honor her great-grandmother for being part of her heritage, but she could also learn from the mistakes her great-grandmother had made. Lucille had valued things more than people, and Cathy wasn't about to follow in those footsteps.

Every time she walked by the oak cabinet, she was assured that the Japanese Tea Set would have a new story, a better story, to tell the generations to come.

18
Teatime with Aunt Eleanor

"Melissa Levinson of Chattanooga has just released her fifth book of afternoon tea recipes, *It's Teatime, Y'all*. The book of southern-themed teatime recipes will be in stores May 12, and a book signing is scheduled at Barnes and Noble for 2 p.m. that afternoon."

No matter how many tea books I'd written, I always enjoyed a new book launch with all its fanfare, especially the book signings and events where I got to meet so many lovely people.

My Aunt Eleanor recently joined the Chattanooga Tea Society, and since she was my favorite aunt, I was happy to oblige when she asked me to speak at their May meeting. Aunt Eleanor was beside herself over getting to host the

meeting and show off her niece with the new tea book.

I promised to bring copies to the meeting, which was held at my aunt's charming Victorian home near downtown. The afternoon of the meeting, I walked up onto the porch and, as always, admired the lush Boston ferns hanging there. Aunt Eleanor had decorated her white wicker porch furniture with needlepoint pillows featuring teacups and teapots. It was going to be a fun afternoon.

When I went inside, Aunt Eleanor proudly introduced "my niece, the author" to her friends, who seemed like sweet ladies. If they were friends of my aunt, that was all I needed to know.

At three o'clock, my aunt signaled it was time for the meeting to begin. My talk, I had been told, was to be short and sweet—fifteen minutes, max—with plenty of time for questions afterward. I loved talking about the history of tea in the United States, particularly about tea cultivation and teatime customs in the South.

Afterward, the women asked some great questions. I knew someone would ask about my favorite tea, Darjeeling, because someone always did, and I also knew someone would ask about the difference between black tea and green tea. My aunt had told her friends about my visit to the tea plantations of India two years ago, so I showed them a few photos of the tea fields, photos I had saved on my iPad for just such show and tell.

At four o'clock, we gathered around the dining table my aunt had elegantly arranged with family silver and floral arrangements. Three-tiered servers were spaced along the table, and tiny vases of fresh flowers were at each place setting, a chalkboard-style tag inscribed with the name of each guest.

My aunt's teenage neighbor, Caroline, helped serve, and she arrived with a tray of what appeared to be piping hot scones. At Aunt Eleanor's urging, Caroline served me first before moving along to the other guests. Once everyone had scones, Aunt Eleanor offered a simple prayer for the meal— she insisted Afternoon Tea was a meal—and then everyone used my aunt's old-fashioned pastry forks to take bites of scones, most of the ladies enjoying the lemon curd and clotted cream as well.

The sound of a fork clanging on china was my first clue these scones weren't quite up to par. Aunt Eleanor had ordered them from a local bakery, and they had assured her that warming them in the oven for a few minutes before teatime would work fine. I knew that was a bad idea the moment I heard it, yet I'd hoped for the best.

I carefully sliced into the scone with my fork. A chunk flew up and hit me in the eye, but I blinked away tears and hoped no one had noticed.

Aiming for a smaller bite, I lightly chipped off a piece of the soft interior, only it wasn't a soft interior. It was raw, and I could see the gummy dough oozing in spots.

Aunt Eleanor said several of the women wanted to see more of my India photos, so while they were busy getting refills of tea, I picked up my napkin, discreetly tucked the rest of my scone into the folds, and headed for the tote bag where I'd stashed my iPad. Napkin in hand, I reached into the bag and pretended to fish around for my iPad while I deposited that dreadful scone.

Several of the women glanced my way, as if they wondered what was taking me so long. I said, "Ah, here it is! Sometimes it gets tangled up in that charger I carry around with it."

When I returned to the table, I was horrified to realize Caroline had placed another scone on my plate.

"Your aunt said you must have enjoyed that other one, so she wanted to make sure you got plenty to eat."

"Oh, my goodness, I'm already getting full. I think I'd better save room for the tea sandwiches and sweets."

"So what do you think of the scones, Melissa?" Aunt Eleanor asked. "I don't eat them anymore since I've gone gluten-free, but the bakery tells me they're some of their most popular items."

Remind me never to eat at that bakery, I thought. "Aren't scones great? I love that legend of the Stone of Scone from over in Scotland. Do you ladies know that story?"

And with that, I went off on a tangent about the history of scones and the many shapes, sizes, and flavors of scones on the market today.

The afternoon passed quickly, and since I had another speaking engagement that evening, I told my aunt I needed to sign books for the friends who wanted one and get on my way. I was pleased when they bought every copy I'd brought.

I was almost out the door when my aunt said, "Caroline, bring that box for Melissa, would you, dear?"

The young helper arrived bearing a plastic-lidded tray filled with scones.

"The rest of these are going home with you, dear, because no one enjoys a good scone as much as you. Isn't that right?" said Aunt Eleanor.

A *good* scone?

"That's absolutely right," I said, giving my aunt a kiss. "Absolutely right."

19
The Mother's Day Tea Mug

"Is my nose really this big?"

I whispered the question to Dan this morning after the boys came in with a tray bearing my Mother's Day gifts, which included a pottery mug supposedly featuring my likeness that David, my six-year-old, made in school, and the breakfast that Jared, my eight-year-old, made in the kitchen. I was already self-conscious about my oversized schnoz, and when I saw the one on my mug from David, I was ready to book that appointment with a plastic surgeon.

Dan assured me he thought my nose was "cute," but I wasn't buying that.

A better mother wouldn't have pondered such things and would have graciously accepted the tray of cereal and burned toast with a smile on her face—which I did—but without thinking, "I wonder how much they wrecked the kitchen?" So I ate the soggy Cheerios, insisted on sharing my toast with Dan, and proved to David that I really did love my new mug by heading into the kitchen and steeping a cup of English Breakfast Tea.

I didn't know where his teacher got the clay or whatever probably toxic substance that thing was made of, but it weighed ten pounds empty, and with tea, a solid fifteen. As soon as I finished sipping, I told David I loved the mug way too much to use it every day, and I plucked a hydrangea blossom from a vase by the kitchen window and voila, a new tea mug vase.

Mother's Day ought to have been renamed National Motherhood Guilt Day. Seriously. Older moms might have enjoyed the day and basked in the adoration of their successful adult children, but those of us with young kids? We knew we'd never be Mother of the Year. I was simply trying to get my boys through elementary school without too many more calls to the principal's office.

And two nights ago, I had just finished doing laundry when Jared ran in yelling that David had something stuck in his cast and couldn't get it out. Yeah. As if a cast wasn't bad enough...

Turned out, David had an itch on his broken leg and wondered if a plastic army man holding a bayonet might relieve his symptoms. He poked the stupid thing so far up his cast that it got stuck and was causing him, apparently, excruciating levels of pain.

I did not enjoy explaining that to the good people on duty at Emergency Care. One of them remembered us from the night David first broke his leg six weeks ago, but then it wasn't every day a kid came in with a leg flopping out from under his Iron Man costume and refusing to let go of his plastic pumpkin full of Halloween candy. In March.

A Year of Teatime Tales

My boys were forever challenging me to research new topics that none of the parenting manuals ever addressed. Forget about the books on teaching kids self-esteem and anti-bullying stuff. I wanted to see a children's book with chapters titled "Places You Do Not Poke Marbles" and "Why We Don't Replace Mommy's Ocean Scent Body Mist with Windex."

This morning before church, I spent twenty minutes trying to figure out what Jared did with the khakis I laid out for him yesterday. They were pressed and draped across his beanbag chair when I kissed him good night, but this morning, there was nothing there. Nada. He hadn't seen the pants. David said he hadn't seen them either, and just to be sure, I looked up his cast, though Dan said that was overkill. So maybe there was a pants thief wandering around the neighborhood and I just hadn't read that e-mail from the homeowners association yet, but I doubted it.

After Sunday School, the boys came out with Mother's Day cards they'd made for me. Jared's was addressed to "World's Best Mom, Amy Simpson." David's was a fill-in-the-blank model from his Sunday School book, and it read, "I love my mom because ..." He'd written, "She makes good tacos sometimes." Sometimes?

The pastor called on all the moms to stand up and be recognized, and I thought—not for the first time—that a gift certificate for babysitting would be a much nicer gift than the carnation and bookmark they gave us Every. Single. Year.

After church, we headed to Dan's mom's for lunch. I called my mom on the way to wish her a Happy Mother's Day. She and my dad were in Hawaii on vacation, and they were about to go snorkeling. Sigh.

Dan's mom loved to cook, hallelujah, and the boys gave her the new Pioneer Woman cookbook, which she appeared to love.

After lunch, we went home, and I got my real gift this year. Dan took the boys to the park for two whole hours. I was going to organize my crafts studio, read my new novel, and wash the boys' ball uniforms for this week's games. Instead, I took a nap.

When I woke up, Dan and the boys were just getting back. He'd gotten a pizza for supper, bless him. A few hours of computer games later, and it was time to tuck the boys in for the night.

Jared was my easy child and always went off to sleep without a fuss. David, this time, was actually kind of quiet—for him—

when I went in to say good night.

"Did you really like your mug, Mom?" David asked.

"Sweetie, I love it," I said. "Didn't you see me drinking tea out of it this morning and then using it as a new vase?"

"Yeah," he said, "but my teacher made all the noses too big. I told her your nose is much smaller than that, and my mug isn't nearly as pretty as you are."

I gave him a kiss, told him I loved him, tucked the Iron Man sheets around him, and headed to the kitchen, where I admired my beautiful new tea mug-slash-vase.

Happy Mother's Day? Yeah, it was.

A Year of Teatime Tales

~ 20 ~
The Chinese Tea Basket

It was Katherine's seventy-fifth birthday, and Mary Linda could hardly wait to present her with a gift.

The two had lived near each other in Atlanta since the time their parents brought them home from the hospital within four days of each other. Katherine was the older girl, and Mary Linda had never let her forget it.

They were fast friends from early on and more like sisters by the time they graduated high school. For that reason, their parents were quite comfortable surprising the girls with a three-week trip to China as a graduation gift. They flew out of New York and were met in Beijing by old family friends, a missionary couple who had agreed to serve as hosts and chaperones.

During their stay, they toured some of the country's many magnificent sites, including the Forbidden City and the Great Wall of China. No matter how busy they were, their hostess served green tea every afternoon, using a beautiful Chinese teapot and matching handleless cups stored in a wicker basket. Katherine and Mary Linda found it the height of sophistication, and both developed a lifelong appreciation for green tea.

Katherine had shopped for a similar set for decades. Once, she thought she'd found it at a small antique shop in Chicago, but the teapot lid had been smashed to smithereens and inexpertly repaired. Perhaps that tea set was supposed to remain a memory.

Their love for teatime wasn't the only thing influenced by that trip. For Katherine, the taste of travel whetted her appetite for more. Once home, she got a receptionist job in a small Atlanta travel agency where she fell in love and married a man who loved to travel as much as she did. Because they both worked in the travel industry, when their children came along, the young family got to enjoy many trips across the United States and abroad.

Mary Linda, meanwhile, had caught the eye of the captain on their flight to Beijing. Phone numbers were swapped, a courtship ensued, and she married him with the understanding she didn't want to leave Atlanta. Since the airport there was getting busier every day, that was not a problem for the young pilot.

The girls' trip to China was just the beginning of their travel adventures. They had enjoyed tea in the shadow of Windsor Castle, had toured the Colosseum in Rome, and had purchased matching Hermès scarves in Paris after visiting the Eiffel Tower. In their seventies, they continued to enjoy trips together, such as the Alaskan cruise they'd just taken with their husbands.

Mary Linda couldn't believe Katherine was about to celebrate such a milestone birthday, and she was only days behind. Seventy-five. How did those years fly by so quickly?

She could tell by the mirror—and by the medicine cabinet—that her body was changing, but inside, she was still that excited eighteen-year-old who flew to China after graduation. She was a little wiser, she hoped, but eternally young where it counted.

One winter day, she and her husband were driving to a family reunion out of state when she spotted a huge, junky-looking antique mall. Something told her to stop.

The place was freezing cold, and Mary Linda shivered as she walked the aisles with a watchful eye. She was ready to head back to the car to warm up when she saw it—a wicker basket fastened with a metal latch and clasp.

Don't get your hopes up, she told herself. How many times had she come across what she thought was a wicker tea basket only to realize it was simply another old purse?

Could it be?

Mary Linda had unhooked the latch, lifted the clasp, raised the lid, and held her breath. Finally! Inside was a set that was a dead ringer for the one she and Katherine had used in China fifty-seven years ago.

The night of Katherine's party, Mary Linda and her husband pulled up at the country club and parked the Cadillac. As she reached into the backseat for the carefully wrapped package, Mary Linda smiled at the bright red rice paper she'd found to wrap the gift. Perfect. Up the steps and into the club she went, eager to find her friend.

The party invitation had expressly said no gifts, but Mary Linda couldn't have cared less about that particular breach of etiquette. The second she saw Katherine, she motioned her over to a small side room at the club, one that was temporarily quiet and empty.

"Come here. Open your gift," she said.

"Gift?" Katherine said. "I thought we agreed we weren't swapping gifts this year."

"I lied," Mary Linda said. "Now go on and open it."

"You've got my curiosity up now," Katherine said, tugging at the paper and tape. She wriggled off the bright red bow and paused to admire the giftwrap.

Mary Linda had used a lot of tissue in the box, so she

knew it would take Katherine a few minutes to unearth the gift. A gasp. A look. And ... was that a tear?

"It can't be," Katherine said. "Not after all this time."

"Yes, it is," Mary Linda said, a deep joy filling her as she watched her best friend admire the same tea accoutrements they had enjoyed as young women on their first travels around the world.

"And just for fun"—Mary Linda reached into her fuchsia floral tote bag—"I brought a Thermos. It's green tea, and I want us to share the first cups using your new tea set."

Tears streamed down Katherine's face, and Mary Linda's wasn't exactly dry.

"I washed the teapot and the cups, by the way," Mary Linda said as Katherine laughed.

Mary Linda poured some still-steaming tea into Katherine's cup and then her own. She held it aloft, urging Katherine to do the same.

"To friendship," she said, gently clinking cups.

"To friendship," Katherine said.

And just as they had all those years before, they sipped and enjoyed their tea.

A Year of Teatime Tales

21
Memories and Memorial Day

After enjoying her first cup of English Breakfast tea, Allison pulled a simple cream-colored teapot from a shelf in one of the kitchen cabinets. She didn't want anything colorful or festive, just a simple teapot to serve as a vase.

She opened the drawer where she kept her pruning shears, grabbed a pair of garden gloves tucked nearby, and

headed out back to her rose garden. Unusual for May, there was a chill in the air, and that suited her just fine.

Her David Austin English roses were doing well, she noticed, especially the soft, vintage pink ones like 'Tea Clipper' and 'Wedgwood.' But no, those frilly specimens weren't the ones she wanted. Only those velvety blood-red American roses would do for the arrangement she had in mind.

Actually, Allison liked all roses. The sturdy red ones out back came with the house, probably some Jackson and Perkins roses bought by the truckload back when the subdivision was first built decades ago. Sturdy and stately, the lush red roses never failed to bloom and give off their sweet perfume.

Allison usually preferred to see her roses on the bushes as God intended them, but that day, she had something else in mind and needed them inside.

Earlier in the year, Allison and her husband, Mark, had vacationed in France for two weeks. While there, they decided to visit the Normandy American Cemetery and Memorial. Mark was a World War II buff, and while Allison was by no means the expert he was, she was only too happy to make the trip because she'd always heard how her great-uncle, Marvin, had died in Normandy on D-Day. She never knew the specifics of his death but simply considered him one of the awful casualties of war.

As a media specialist—what they called a "librarian" back when she was in school—Allison knew the basic timeline of the war, the major battles, and the historic moments that were still taught to most students. Her trip to Normandy, however, convinced her how much she had yet to learn about the war.

One of Mark's old college friends, Gerard, lived near Colleville-sur-Mer, the town where the cemetery was located, and he had met Mark and Allison at the nearest train station and driven them to the site. The entrance was beautifully landscaped. Simply going through the visitor center was a moving experience. There, portraits showed some of those who died in the war, including a woman who had the same name as a teacher at Allison's school. That was rather jarring to her, as it no doubt was for that woman's friends all those years ago.

But it was an offhand comment Gerard had made in the visitor center that stayed with Allison.

She had been studying the grainy old photos of young men landing on Omaha Beach when she noted the heavy equipment they were carrying as they left their landing craft and headed to shore.

"It's a wonder they made it through the water with those heavy loads," she said.

"Many of them didn't," Gerard said. "Lots of them drowned before they ever even got to shore."

Allison had always assumed her great-uncle was killed by a land mine or gunfire on D-Day. It never occurred to her he might have drowned.

After touring the cemetery and viewing all the memorials, she realized there was a lot about World War II that had never occurred to her.

"Whatcha doing?" Mark asked, suddenly interrupting Allison's reverie.

"Oh, nothing. Just making a little flower arrangement for our Memorial Day cookout," she said.

"Listen, I'm running to the store for more gas for the grill. I don't want to run out while your family's here this evening."

"Sounds good," she said and watched him leave. Grilling out on Memorial Day was one of her favorite family traditions.

As Allison pulled a spotty leaf from one of her roses, she thought back to the flower arrangements she had seen lying at the base of some of the crosses and Stars of David marking those graves in Normandy. She had placed a small bouquet at her great-uncle's grave. Like other visitors to the cemetery, she and Mark had gathered sand from the beach and rubbed it into the engraved lettering on the cross so that Marvin's name would show up in a photo. Afterward, she'd wondered whether it was respectful to take a photo of a grave marker, yet she couldn't have imagined not taking the photo. She was glad she had, because her parents had seemed to appreciate it.

Enjoying the quiet and peaceful morning, Allison was content to be back home in America, traipsing through her rose garden and snipping roses.

For far too many years, she thought, she had treated Memorial Day as simply a fun holiday and an excuse for a three-day weekend. But the trip to Normandy had changed that. It made her resolve to observe the day properly and remember those who gave their lives for their country—including her great-uncle.

Satisfied with her rose selections, Allison went back inside the house to preheat the oven for a cake she was baking for the family cookout. Then she prepared another cup of tea and settled in to watch the news, hoping perhaps someone would be filming live at the cemetery in Normandy. The sight of those 9,387 grave markers was one she would never forget. And she hoped she'd never again take it lightly.

Allison rinsed out the cream teapot, filled it halfway full with cool water, and arranged a few of those deep red roses. In back, she added a small American flag she'd picked up at the craft store.

"There," she said. "And thank you, Uncle Marvin."

A Year of Teatime Tales

~ 22 ~
The Secret Diary of a Garden Party Attendee

Dear Diary,

    Just once before I die, I would love to have a garden party on the lawn that wasn't attended by eight thousand of my closest friends. Today, I stood on my feet for two solid hours and shook hand after hand and gave smile after smile. It does wear upon one.

Oh, I know I'm not supposed to feel this way, and it's a privilege I enjoy because of my birthright, but the truth of the matter is that I'm getting a little old for this sort of thing. I can't publicly say this, of course, because the gossip rags already have us dead every time Philip or I come down with a sniffle.

The English people love these garden parties, though, so attend them I must.

At least I had an especially nice outfit this time. My dressmaker never lets me down, bless her soul. The bright pink color of my coat and hat had the press wagging about how it was clearly a reference to William and Kate's new daughter, Charlotte. It's fine with me if everyone wants to believe I wore pink because of that, but the truth is, I liked the color, and when my stylist suggested it, I said it would be fine. The happy color made me look a little perkier than I felt.

And speaking of color, I could hardly believe that green and purple jacket Anne wore to the party. Good heavens, I haven't seen that many flowers on a fabric since my late mother had her drawing room furniture reupholstered back in the eighties. I've never quite understood where my daughter gets her fashion sense, but at least I never have to worry about her behavior. Goodness knows I haven't always been able to say that about *every* member of this family.

My granddaughter Beatrice, I'm proud to report, was at the garden party and looked lovely in her very modest dress and jacket, and she represented the firm quite nicely. I can tell she gets tired of all the pleasantries herself and would no doubt prefer to be at the club, polishing off a few cocktails with her chums, but she knows how to plaster a smile on her face and make the expected small talk. Andrew and Sarah have done a fine job with those two girls, and in fact, I so wish he and Sarah would … well, no, I promised myself I would keep my nose out of that business, didn't I?

Philip is so good to accompany me on these social occasions, and goodness knows he's had a lifetime to get used to them. The man never complains about the garden parties, but I could tell he was itching to get inside and go back to playing Candy Crush. Those poor souls on Facebook have no idea who "Princely Dude" is, do they?

I still find it rather shocking that people will line up for hours just to sip a few cups of tea and eat a few cucumber sandwiches and slices of cake, all for the chance to curtsy or bow to me and possibly shake my hand.

Thank goodness everyone is used to seeing me wear gloves. With all those dreadful diseases spreading around the world today, I can only imagine what I would end up with if I didn't have my trusty gloves on. I haven't been seriously ill in years, so I think they must help. Let the Americans keep those little squirt bottles of hand sanitizer they're so fond of. Gloves. That's the trick.

And while all the chitchat gets old fast, I do, however, enjoy talking with the older citizens who show up at these parties. The social climbers, not so much, but the elderly, I have a real soft spot for. Today, there was a delightful ninety-seven-year-old woman in a wheelchair. She said she'd been waiting her entire life simply for the chance to see me up close, and now she could die happy since she'd gotten to shake my hand. She said it was the happiest moment of her life. I hardly feel worthy of such admiration.

So yes, the lovely old people make it a somewhat worthwhile occasion, and so, year after year, I ask that, yet again, the wait staff pour more tea and prepare more slices of cake.

I still think it would be great fun just to have a small party on the lawn one day for, oh, a few family members, like William and Kate and the children, Harry—as long as he's not dating a hooker at the moment—Andrew and Sarah, and ... oops, there I go again!

One reason I have ordered these diaries to be destroyed once I'm gone is that everyone would think me such a whiner if they knew how I truly felt about so many of these social obligations. And there are those who would be shocked at what I genuinely think about my family, for that matter.

Besides phoning up a few of my cousins, where else can I say what I *really* think about Anne's jacket?

Well, Dear Diary, it's time to call it a day. All that standing and greeting has gotten to this old gal.

Besides that, Philip keeps trying to get me to play at least one game of Candy Crush. He's signed me up for an account under the name "Queenie," the silly old fool.

Till next time,

ER

23
The Mostly True Story of Shen Nung

"They think I'm an idiot."

"No, they do not, my lord. It simply isn't possible."

"Don't tell me that! I know when I'm being ridiculed!"

"It's a simple misunderstanding, my lord. I'll see that it's cleared up at once."

"See that you do! If I hear that ridiculous tale one more time, somebody is going to be sleeping with the fishes tonight. Do I make myself clear?"

"Yes, my lord."

After bowing to his enraged master, the terrified servant backed up and dashed away.

Despite having sipped his fifth cup of tea that morning, Shen Nung was feeling irritable. It had been ten years since he had discovered the amazing tea plant. A lifelong student of botany, the emperor had sampled hundreds of herbs before the day he came across a tea plant, examined its leaves, observed the plants growing around it, and realized it was probably safe to infuse some leaves in boiling water. He had sipped the resulting brew and taken note of how his body responded, how calm and yet alert he felt upon sipping the beverage.

But to his dismay, after ten fine years of sharing the glories of tea with others, his careful discovery of tea was most assuredly *not* the story that was getting around.

Shen Nung seemed destined to be remembered as that foolhardy emperor who was idling away the hours in the woods one day when some tea leaves landed in a nearby pot of boiling water and magically steeped themselves. How, he wondered, could anyone think a pot of boiling water just happened to appear out in the woods?

He had brought agriculture to China, and he was so well versed in herbs that he ultimately tasted some three hundred and sixty-five of them. Did his subjects think it was purely by accident that he had sampled an herb for every day of the year? For that matter, did they even know about the extent of his work with herbs?

No. Instead, the story spreading faster than wildfire was that Shen Nung, like a simpleton, was sitting outdoors one day near a cauldron of boiling water—such an unlikely scenario in and of itself—when some tea leaves just happened to drift by, just happened to land in the pot, and he just happened to observe them and decided to taste the resulting brew. It was enough to drive an emperor mad.

"What if that had been a poisonous plant?" he had asked his poor servant the first time he heard the so-called legend being repeated about him.

"Then, my lord, I don't suppose you would be here having this conversation," the servant had cautiously replied.

"Indeed not!" the emperor said.

His library was full of notations about the plants he had studied. He had nearly lost his eyesight because of his exacting studies of the tea plant and the minute details he had captured in both word and art.

One of the emperor's favorite servants had tried to assure him that history would recall him with fondness.

"My lord, even if the tale gets told for thousands of years, they will always remember that you were the one who discovered tea. Imagine the pleasure this beverage will give to men down through the ages, and how fitting it will be that such an astute man as yourself will be remembered always for this fine gift."

The emperor had considered his servant's wise words. The man was right, of course. Tea drinking was already a popular pastime in his kingdom, and Shen Nung wondered if perhaps one day it would spread to other areas of the country as well.

The emperor grew accustomed to hearing the "legend" of how he had discovered tea, and he had devised the perfect plan for correcting the record, although he realized that his plan unfortunately would not reach fruition until his death.

Many years later, as he lay dying, Shen Nung wrote the true account of how he studied the tea plant and introduced it to the world. In his careful handwriting, he outlined precisely how he had discovered the tea plant and how it was by no means a purely accidental discovery. Because that record would be so crucial in establishing the truth, he took time to make sure each word he inked could be read clearly and completely.

One night, however, he woke with a fever, one his family believed was the result of a toxic plant he had chewed on earlier that week, a choice that would prove fatal.

While Shen Nung had recorded for posterity that he had deliberately tried those tea leaves, his attempt at altering his own history was waylaid when an ache in his side made him pounce from the bed and search for a place to empty the contents of his lurching stomach. He leaped from his bed so quickly that he spilled the cup of tea on his bedside table, and the liquid quickly soaked the papers he had been writing, smearing and destroying his tea testimonial for the ages.

Hearing the hubbub in the room, a young servant new to the emperor's service came running and asked, "My lord, what is wrong? How may I help?"

"Tea ..." Shen Nung said. "Tell them about the tea ..." Gasping, Shen Nung pointed at the soggy pile of papers and breathed his last.

His servant, who knew not the true story of tea's discovery, was greatly grieved over his master's death.

"His last words," claimed the dutiful servant, "were for me to make sure the world knows about tea, and I've heard that our great emperor accidentally discovered tea when he was out meditating in the woods one day. I shall devote the rest of my life to making sure the entire world forever associates tea with the name of Shen Nung."

And he did just that.

24
The Pleasure of a Letter

Andrea was standing at the kitchen window and sorting through the day's mail when she saw an envelope with a familiar address label. The sunny yellow teapot on the label told her the letter was from Cindy, her pen pal in New Jersey.

Alabama had been Andrea's home for all of her fifty-eight years, and she and Cindy had been pen pals for twenty of them. Many years ago, they had both been readers of *Romantic Living* magazine when it ran a feature on the joys of pen pals. *Romantic Living* readers wrote in asking for pen pals of their own, so the magazine decided to play matchmaker and assigned pen pals to hundreds of women across the country who were seeking kindred spirits.

At first, the two wondered what they could possibly have in common. Andrea was a newly divorced mother with a young daughter she was raising on her own. Cindy was a happily married mother of four boys whose life seemed to revolve around ballgames and scouts.

But as fans of *Romantic Living* magazine, they weren't surprised to find they did have quite a few things in common. They both loved the color yellow, roses, and teatime. They both enjoyed the ocean more than the mountains, and they both loved their cats.

For Andrea, who worked in sales for a large cable provider, it was nice to have a friend whose focus was more on family than business. For Cindy, who'd been a homemaker all her life, it was fun to hear about office life from a woman who was focusing on her career even more since her daughter, Shannon, had become an adult.

Looking at the pretty cursive handwriting on the new letter, Andrea wondered what tidbits she would find inside. As always, she made a cup of tea before she sat down to read the latest news. Andrea even had a special teacup she used on those days when a new letter arrived. The Wedgwood teacup bore images of the handwriting of Wedgwood company forebear Josiah Wedgwood, a switch from the vintage bone china teacups she usually favored. Sipping tea from that teacup always put her in a nostalgic mood as she read an old-fashioned handwritten letter.

Though Andrea occasionally flew to New Jersey on business, she and Cindy had never met face to face. They had almost met once, during one of Andrea's longer business trips, but one of Cindy's boys had ended up in the hospital with a ruptured appendix, so naturally that emergency took top priority.

After measuring two teaspoons of Darjeeling tea leaves into her single-serve teapot, Andrea added boiling water from the electric teakettle and set her timer for four minutes. Her tabby, Lincoln, came through and brushed against her leg. As Andrea waited for her tea to steep, she wondered what was new with Cindy. Her letters were usually full of chatty news about the boys, her husband, Bill, or perhaps what was going on over at the Catholic church they attended, which Andrea knew was located next to Cindy's home.

Pouring her cup of tea, Andrea thought about all she and Cindy had shared in their letters over the years. In those pages, they had discussed the horror of 9/11, the volatile economy, and the changing political landscape in America. They had discussed marriage, for Cindy, and dating after fifty, for Andrea, and they loved to discuss favorite books and TV programs, especially *Downton Abbey*.

Andrea knew more about Cindy's boys than some of their own family did. Cindy, likewise, had been surprised to learn that Andrea found some of the women she worked with too competitive and had a hard time trusting some of them enough to become close friends.

Andrea sat down at the kitchen table, sipped her tea, and used her letter opener—one she ordered from *Romantic Living* years ago—to unseal the letter. She read:

"Dear Andrea, What does October 3 look like for you? Bill's company has their annual convention in Birmingham that weekend, and if you can fit me in, I'm going to go, too, and skip the convention to spend time with you!"

Cindy was traveling to Birmingham? Andrea couldn't believe it. She could hardly wait for her pen pal to visit, and what was even better, that was the weekend the Friends of the Library held their annual fall tea, so she and Cindy could attend together.

Or maybe Cindy would like to visit one of the area's tearooms instead. Or would she prefer a visit to the botanical garden? The gardens were still pretty at that time of year, and Cindy did love to garden ...

Andrea caught herself before she started daydreaming any further, and she read the rest of Cindy's letter. It went on to report that Mark was about to graduate from college with his degree in business, Jason had gotten a job in digital marketing with a home improvement chain based in New Jersey, and the twins, Luke and Leo, had both broken an arm while playing baseball, although the injuries were three days apart.

The last of the Darjeeling gone from her teacup, Andrea

sat and smiled at the letter with the pretty handwriting. Would she finally get to meet the woman she'd swapped countless letters with? She would have to do much planning to make it the most wonderful trip imaginable.

"Dear Cindy, October 3 now has a big red smiley face on it on my kitchen calendar! Yes to October 3, and please tell me you'll stay here at the house. I've been wanting to show off the new guest room for months, but so far the only ones who've visited have been some of Shannon's roommates. How often would you like to go to tea while you're here, because …"

Andrea put down her pen and had to smile. It had all started, innocently enough, with a simple letter.

25
Times Remembered

Lynn woke and, realizing what day it was, closed her eyes and pulled the sheet up over her head. Maybe she could sleep a few more minutes and postpone the inevitable. But after tossing and turning for ten minutes, she went ahead and got up from the guest bedroom at her father's house. It was the day she and her brothers were going to move him into assisted living.

Her father, Charles, was doing well physically, but mentally, he'd been slipping for months.

At first, the dementia wasn't so noticeable. Lynn had stopped by one day around lunchtime to the smell of scorched food coming from the kitchen. "Dad, is something burning?" she had asked. Rushing into her father's small kitchen, Lynn had discovered a tomato soup can on the counter and a small saucepan with the burned remains of soup clinging to the bottom and sides.

Her father claimed he had simply gotten busy watching *Gunsmoke* and forgotten to turn off the soup. Later, he claimed he was distracted because he was thinking about how much he missed his late wife. That excuse might have worked if she hadn't passed away twenty-six years before.

Lynn and her twin brothers, Richard and Russell, all lived nearby and tried to check on their father often, but it had gotten to the point that "often" wasn't enough. One evening about nine, her dad's neighbor, Mrs. Barnes, called.

"Honey, I don't want to worry you, but your father was just outside in his boxers and a T-shirt, watering the azaleas. I got him to go back inside, but he seemed confused about what time it was, so you might want to come check on him."

After seeing both her teenage daughters off to college the previous fall, Lynn had looked forward to a year of carefree living, maybe taking a class at the community college or finally joining a book group. She hadn't realized that parenting a parent was going to be one of the hardest jobs she'd ever had. To top it off, she felt guilty for even thinking about herself when her father was clearly in decline.

She and her brothers had been preparing for the move for weeks. They had tidied up the neat red brick ranch-style house, knowing eventually they would have to put it on the market, and one of the three spent the night at their father's house every night. Charles knew something was up, and it was making him nervous.

The three siblings had agreed they all wanted to be there when their father left the house to go to his new home. Lynn went into her father's bedroom and gathered some of his personal items and toiletries, just the few things he would need to help him settle in at Grayson Manor. The assisted living director had advised her not to bring any of her father's valuables with him, but he didn't have many valuables at that point. He still wore his watch and his wedding ring, but that was about it.

Lynn did a fast check of the worn wooden tray where her father had always kept his watch, his spare change, and his wallet. A small wooden box contained a photo of her late mother along with a few other mementos. He would want that photo for sure, and to Lynn's surprise, when she reached inside the box, there sat the gaudy, tarnished old teapot pin he had purchased for Lynn when she was a little girl.

Lynn wandered back in time to the late fifties. She and her father had gone to a Father-Daughter Tea at church on the Saturday before Father's Day. That afternoon, her father took her to Woolworth's to select a memento to mark the occasion. When Lynn spotted the rhinestone pin, she had insisted that was what she wanted. Lynn's father had tried to talk her into getting a nice charm bracelet instead, since those were so popular with girls back then, but Lynn had been adamant about getting that gaudy rhinestone pin. Lynn hadn't thought of that old pin in years. On a whim, she fastened the piece onto the crisp cotton blouse she'd worn that morning.

When she walked back into the living room, her father was watching *Gunsmoke*. He loved that show, and every week or so he asked if the actor who played Festus was still alive.

Suddenly, her father looked her way and got a big smile on his face.

"What is it, Dad?"

"That's the pin you got that time you went to tea with me right before Father's Day."

"I know, Dad."

Lynn was amazed that her father could, on occasion, still remember something like that—yet he couldn't remember to take his medication at breakfast. Maybe her father was doing better than she thought.

Lynn went into the kitchen and poured herself a glass of iced tea. She hoped they made good iced tea at the assisted living place, because that was all her father would drink with his dinner. She walked back into the living room and joined him on the sofa.

Charles looked at her, again staring at the teapot pin on her blouse.

"That's a pretty pin, sweetheart," he said. "Is that new?"

Lynn swallowed. "No, Dad. It's just"—her fingers flew to the satiny gold surface of the pin—"something I've had for a while," she said.

There was a knock at the door, and Lynn opened it to find Richard and Russell standing there, looking just as nervous as she felt.

"Are we ready?" asked Richard.

Russell, who had always been closest to their dad, looked on the verge of tears.

"Yes," Lynn said. "It's time."

She touched the teapot pin again, recalled the happy memories of the past, and told herself that maybe there was still time to make a few more.

26
The Vintage Iced Tea Pitcher

A summer thunderstorm had knocked the power out, and the thermostat showed it'd already crept up to seventy-nine in the living room. Fortunately, I had just poured myself a glass of iced tea, and that was what I sipped as I sat on the porch.

It was still humid after that storm. Steam rose off the asphalt at the end of our driveway, and tree branches and leaves carpeted the path of the utility truck that had just pulled up at the Wilsons' house down the street. I hoped we'd have electricity again soon.

I held my glass up to my forehead and pretended its cold, icy surface was an ice pack.

"Ellen, what're you doing?"

"Cooling off, which I highly recommend," I told Mark as he headed up the driveway. I knew he was about to go investigate that utility truck.

I held the glass in place a moment, then looked at the pretty pink flowers on it and smiled. I remembered the day I found that pitcher and iced tea glasses ...

Since I taught seventh graders nine months out of the year, those summer days of freedom and no five a.m. wake-up alarms were precious indeed.

That Friday morning, I left home and stopped by Starburnt—as Mark always called it—for a cup of chai and a scone, then got on the interstate and headed north.

Soon, I spotted a billboard for the "South's Largest Indoor Flea Market." That would've been more impressive if I hadn't visited before, because I knew the place was heavy on the fleas, light on the markets.

Next, I saw a sign advertising "Mega Antique Mall, 200+ Booths." The sign said it was just a few exits farther, and I needed to stop for gas anyway, so I got off there and followed the signs to the mega mall—only to find that it was mega closed. Sheets of plywood were nailed where the doors once stood. Back to the car, back to the interstate. I'd give it one more shot before heading home.

The next billboard had a name I'd never seen before: "Benson's Antiques—Exit 117—Something for Everyone." I got there in twenty minutes.

When I pulled up, I saw that Benson's appeared to be open, which I took as a good sign.

Benson's was no mega mall. The antiques were apparently sold in a rickety old Victorian house, its wraparound porch cluttered with rotting wicker, iron plant stands, and oak dressers with broken mirrors.

Opening the front door, I peeked into what looked like hoarder heaven. I glanced around for the owner but spotted no one, so I started browsing the dusty tables piled high with cardboard boxes.

Some old magazines caught my eye. One issue had a 1965 Thunderbird on the cover. Mark's 1965 Thunderbird was his pride and joy, so I got him that magazine, which was only a dollar. I tucked it under my arm and headed to the next room.

Surprisingly, the room had wall-to-wall shelves brimming with china and glassware. Whoever owned Benson's obviously collected Depression glass, based on the many shelves of green and yellow plates, glasses, and bowls. Prices were low, too—Depression glass pitchers for twelve dollars, bone china teacups and saucers for eight dollars.

Scouring the shelves for something special, I spotted a vintage pitcher and glasses with pink and red flowers. I'd seen a set like that once and coveted it, but it was sixty dollars—too much. Benson's set was just twenty. Was something wrong with it? I ran my finger along the rims of the glasses and pitcher but found no flaws.

If only a "Benson" were there to take my money.

I wandered into the next room, which was packed with linens and kitchenwares. I'd never seen so many canister sets before—roosters, cows, mushrooms.

From the front of the house came the sound of the creaky front door opening, so I walked back up front, hoping to find the owner.

There stood a large, black-haired woman with a bouffant hairstyle and eyes heavily rimmed in black liner. She wore a fuchsia and green maxi dress, and bangle bracelets clanged on both arms. She was balancing two giant Styrofoam cups as she tried to close the door with her hip.

"Let me help you," I said, rushing over and closing the door.

"Thanks," she said brightly. "Sorry I wasn't here to welcome you, but I had to run to the store for some sweet tea. It's so hot this morning, and nothing cools you off like sweet tea. You like tea?"

"Love it," I said. "Had some on the way here." I didn't bother to explain that mine was hot chai.

"Good," she said. "Then you won't mind if I sip my tea while you look around."

"Actually, I was ready to check out," I said, "but please, go on and drink your tea."

"B'lieve I will," she said, taking a big slurp and fanning herself with an old copy of *McCall's* before she began to write up my sales ticket.

Jackie—as she introduced herself—wanted to know where I was from, what I collected, and what I planned to do with her old tea pitcher. She'd been in the antiques business for decades and liked to make sure her merchandise went to good homes. She carefully wrapped my purchases in newspapers she'd been saving since President Reagan was in office.

When I thanked her and told her to have a nice day, she waved me off with a cheery "B'lieve I will."

What a character, and what a fun day ...

Mark walked down the driveway, looking satisfied.

"What's the verdict?"

"Should be back on in about—"

The hum of the electricity turning on reached our ears at the same moment.

"Want to head back inside?" Mark asked, holding the door.

I looked at my iced tea glass and decided it was time for a refill.

"B'lieve I will," I said.

A Year of Teatime Tales

27
Tomato Sandwich
Freedom Day

"Hurry up, Joe, and pass the mayonnaise."
"Don't get your boxers in a bundle, Art," I say. "I'm gonna enjoy these tomato sandwiches, and I don't mean to be rushed."

Art's wife, Patricia, and my wife, Barb, are best friends, and the four of us have been going to the Gulf Coast together for years. We probably ought to have our heads examined for always going the week before the Fourth of July. It's crowded, it's hot, it's expensive—and we couldn't stop now if we tried.

Today's the day Patricia and Barb have gone to the outlet mall an hour away, or as Art and I like to think of it, Tomato Sandwich Freedom Day.

Art and I love good old-fashioned tomato sandwiches, but unfortunately, we are both married to health fanatics. Barb would bring anthrax into our house before she'd permit a loaf of white bread to enter. So most of the year, I eat that wretched brown stuff she buys in the organic section at the grocery store. My cholesterol's down, and the doctor's happy I've lost ten pounds, but he'd lose weight, too, if his wife made him eat bread with sand and dirt in it.

Patricia's even worse. That woman can tell you the calorie, sodium, and carb count of every bite of food she puts in her mouth, and she rides Art's case all the time. Art's about twenty pounds overweight thanks to those all-you-can-eat buffet lunches he has about three or four times a week, but if I had to live like that, I'd probably be a regular at Golden Corral too.

Today, however, Art and I are two free men, and we've just gotten back from Winn-Dixie, where we stocked up on provisions before the gals return.

We do this every year at the beach, and the grocery list is always the same—the biggest loaf of Sunbeam white bread we can find, a big jar of Duke's mayonnaise, store brand salt and pepper, and tomatoes from the closest vegetable stand.

This year, I've added to the feast by making something that would drive Patricia nuts if she were here—a gallon of sweet tea made with two whole cups of white sugar.

The condo has a kitchenette, and when we were at the grocery store, I recalled seeing a stack of saucepans under one of the cabinets. I boiled water in the pan, added Lipton tea bags like we had when I was a kid, and then I let that beautiful white sugar melt right down in it all. I poured it straight into a big old Mason jar, added a bunch of those little half-moons of ice, and took a swig. Ah.

"You got tomato seeds dribbling down your shirt, pal," I tell Art.

"Don't care," he says, taking another bite. "I'll change before Patricia gets back."

"Humph," I say, enjoying another bite of my sandwich, the soft and gooey white bread sticking to the roof of my mouth. Man, the tomatoes are good this year.

Barb and Patricia buy these little bitty organic tomatoes the size of a quarter and talk about how tasty they are, but they can't compete with these juicy Big Boys. I slice mine a little thinner than Art does, but shoot, I don't care how he slices his tomatoes as long as he leaves mine alone.

Art doesn't get to eat Duke's the rest of the year, but I do. That man is so henpecked, it's pitiful. I promised Barb I'd try to eat healthy, but I refuse to eat fake mayonnaise. Life's too short, and like my mama always said, none of us came to stay. What's the point in adding another decade or two to life if you've got to spend it eating sorry mayonnaise?

Art and Patricia eat some kind of "heart healthy" mayonnaise that triggers my gag reflex just to think about it.

I polish off my first sandwich and get going on the second. I know I'm probably good for a third. Besides, Art and I'll be on a fishing boat soon, and we'll sweat off a few calories.

Tonight, we're going to some fancy new seafood restaurant the girls heard about. Barb and Patricia will probably order broiled shrimp and chef salads, but if Art and I want surf and turf, or baked potatoes with every single topping on the menu, that's what we'll get.

How'd we get our wives to go along with that? Easy.

One year, Barb and Patricia wanted to go to the outlet mall. They'd been nagging us about our diets all the way down to the beach and said they were afraid to leave us alone at the condo, so they suggested Art and I join them for a little shopping. I said I thought that was a great idea.

"Have you lost your mind, Joe?" Art had muttered under his breath.

"Trust me," I'd told him.

That day, we stuck to our wives like chewing gum to the bottom of a shoe. Every time one of 'em picked up something, we commented on it. Every time they found a "bargain," Art or I mentioned how expensive this vacation was and how we needed to watch the household budget. When Barb looked at a new set of cookware, I just smiled and said I thought our old cookware was just fine.

Interestingly enough, Art and I never got invited back shopping with them again, and they never said another word about our vacation eating habits.

"You gonna share that can of Pringles or do I need to head back to Winn-Dixie and buy some more?" I ask Art.

"Here you go. Knock yourself out. And Joe, that was a great idea about the sweet tea. Man, this reminds me of eating tomato sandwiches at my grandmother's house when I was a boy."

"I know what you mean," I say. "Pour me another glass of that tea, will ya?"

Mmm, mmm, mmm.

A Year of Teatime Tales

28
Just Because

"Ellen Wilson, Occupant." "Ellen Wilson, Homeowner." "Ellen Wilson, Gardener."

Ellen wondered how the direct mail companies decided how to address the junk mail they sent her way. That morning, following a recent trip to the Container Store, she was enjoying a much-anticipated day of cleaning and purging. She was tossing old bills, magazine offers, and pretty much any piece of paper that wasn't absolutely necessary to running the household.

Why didn't the mail ever bring a *nice* surprise sometime? *For that matter, why don't I send a nice surprise sometime?*

Ellen wasn't quite sure where the thought came from. She'd planned to spend the morning cleaning her home office and tidying up, yet she had a sudden but very strong impression to stop what she was doing and send a gift to her friend Lisa. She knew just the thing to send. Ellen had been downsizing her china collection, and she had a teacup with pink roses on it that Lisa loved.

In the middle of her morning's busyness, Ellen stopped what she was doing, packaged up the teacup for her friend, and included a note that read simply "Just Because." The two had long had a habit of doing things for each other for no reason or any reason, and their "Just Because" gifts were one way the two friends had managed to stay in touch.

Ellen wasn't quite sure why she felt such a strong urge to send Lisa something that morning, but she did. She drove to the post office, sent the package on its way, and returned home to continue climbing Mount Junk Mail.

Three days later ...

Lisa Andrews was having a bad day. First, her blow dryer died while she was getting ready for work. It gave a rumbling sound followed by the distinct smell of electrical unhappiness, and Lisa's hair was only halfway dried. She combed the damp hair back and pinned it in place, artfully applying gel and hair spray to try to make herself look more presentable.

The marketing company where she worked had a leadership team meeting that morning, and Lisa—rumored to be up for a promotion—was hoping to make a good impression on the company vice president who would be visiting. The "bad hair" impression was not the one she wanted to make.

She was confident in her skill as a marketer, and Lisa knew deep inside that she was worth so much more than how she looked on any given day, but still ... the woman in her wanted to look nice at the meeting. She was headed out the door when she remembered to wear her lucky heart necklace, the one she'd often worn on important days and to important events. When she got to her car, she discovered the clasp had broken and the necklace had dropped into her bra. Lovely.

On the way to work, Lisa told herself that just because her hair and jewelry were having a bad day didn't mean that she had to. She hit the interstate for the twenty-five-minute drive to the office and determined to give her best at the meeting.

About a mile up the interstate, she hit the brakes when she saw a sea of red taillights before her. Roadwork? Thank goodness she always left a half hour early. She'd forgotten they were repaving that section of interstate, and a sign told her to expect delays. After five minutes of waiting, she started to get nervous. After ten minutes, she called the office and told the receptionist she might be late. When she was still sitting in traffic fifteen minutes later, she let go of any hopes of having a good day after all. It wasn't going to happen.

When Lisa finally got to the office forty-seven minutes late for her meeting, she learned the vice president had left after just twenty minutes, so she wouldn't get to see him after all. Maybe it was just as well.

Her day didn't get any better. At lunchtime, she stopped by a drive-through, intending to grab something she could eat back at the office. When she opened what was supposed to be her chicken sandwich, she saw they'd given her fish instead. She was allergic to fish.

Around five, Lisa's husband called to report he had a dead battery and wouldn't be home in time to make their reservation at that new restaurant after all. In no hurry, Lisa took a back road home only to find an accident had brought traffic to a standstill. She sat in traffic for the second time that day.

When she finally got home, Lisa couldn't wait to shed her suit and heels and have a cup of tea and maybe watch a movie.

To her surprise, a package sat by the front door. It was from her friend Ellen, who lived a couple of hours away. The two had met when they worked for the same company right out of school, and they'd been friends ever since. Ellen had a home-based business processing insurance claims, and she loved it.

Lisa took the package inside and carefully opened it. Hiding in the bubble wrap was a beautiful pink teacup with roses on it. It was one of the prettiest ones she'd ever seen—and she knew that because she had admired it at Ellen's house for years. Ellen had joked that one day, she'd tire of it and send it Lisa's way.

How interesting that it arrived today. Her friend must have had a feeling Lisa would need a little pick-me-up, and that beautiful teacup certainly did the trick.

After changing into jeans and a comfy T-shirt, Lisa went to the kitchen and prepared her favorite tea, a new Keemun from Harney and Sons. The first sip relaxed her instantly.

She fingered the pretty teacup and admired its cheerful pink flowers. Yes, it had been a bad day, but she certainly didn't have a bad life. Not at all.

29
Power to the Pot

Come here. Lean a little closer. Shhh. I have a secret. Don't tell everyone, but … it's kind of fun being a teapot!

Several years ago, some lady came out with a book called *If Teacups Could Talk*. I thought to myself, "What do you mean *if*?" Everyone knows teacups can talk, but meaning no offense, who *cares* if teacups can talk? Bunch of amateurs. Now teapots, *we* are the ones who have something to say.

Teacups are like commoners, but a teapot is like the Queen. Think about it. You go to a tea party and everybody gets a teacup, but there's usually only one teapot on the table. And oh, the stories I can tell!

I have the best day job in the world. All I have to do is sit there and look pretty until I'm called up for "work," and then I'm usually sitting smack-dab in the middle of a tea party, which is always fun. Why?

First, my owner, Leslie, warms me up before she uses me. She rinses me out with a bit of warm water, and it's like I've gone for a brief swim at some nice Caribbean beach. Makes me feel all ticklish inside just to think about it.

Then, Leslie fills me with warm water to get me ready to serve. I always like that part best because it feels like I'm taking a nice, relaxing bath. If only I could get her to add a few bath salts, but I understand why she doesn't.

Last, she pours in the boiling water and adds the tea bags. Now not everyone is cut out to handle boiling water, but I am. I really strut my stuff then, letting those tea bags know who's boss while they toss around inside me.

"Hey, Earl Grey? What do you think you're doing? Untangle yourself and get back on your side. She'll want you out of here in about four minutes!"

Misbehaving tea bags are another story, and I don't have time to get into that today.

Once the tea bags are out, Leslie makes sure I don't have any drips—kind of like a lady checking for lipstick smears—and takes me to the table. The things I have seen and heard at the tea table ... You'd be surprised. Really, you would.

Sometimes, it's all sweetness and light. Maybe it's a bunch of middle-aged friends getting together to reminisce about their high school days, back before they met Miss Clairol and had to sign up for Zumba classes, if you get my drift.

Other times, a young bride or mother-to-be is the guest at tea, and I really, really enjoy those parties.

You hear the best gossip, though, at the ordinary tea parties where it's just a few close friends getting together for a gabfest.

You want to know what I heard not long ago? You won't believe this.

Leslie was hosting a tea party for three of her girlfriends, and her friend Sharon was there. The other two friends were Diane and Grace, as I recall.

Now I love my owner, but Lord help her, Leslie often speaks before she thinks. So Sharon was sharing a sweet memory and casually mentioned an old friend named Julie. Leslie pipes up with, "Julie? Julie? I don't remember you having any friend named Julie."

I was watching all this play out from right there in the middle of the dining room table, keep in mind.

And then Leslie says, "Oh, wait a minute! Julie! Wasn't she the one whose body they found in a trunk at the airport? The smell got so bad that someone complained, and that's how police found her body?"

You could almost hear the air whooshing out of the room.

"Yes," Sharon had replied, looking a little amused and yet sad all at the same time. "She's the one."

I remember wishing I could speak aloud at the tea so I could say, "Exactly how many dead-body-found-at-the-airport friends do you think Sharon has, Leslie?"

Fortunately, my owner realized her faux pas and soon got the conversation back on track.

I never get an invitation in the mail as the other guests do, yet I must say I enjoy attending tea parties. You never know what you'll overhear, and as a writer, I'm always looking for a good story idea.

(What? You didn't think teapots had hobbies just like anyone else?)

And although my job is simply to hold the tea, I have to tell you that I don't mind admitting I sip a little of the brew myself once the others are served. Oolongs are my favorite, but at tea parties, I inevitably get asked to hold some fruity tea like strawberry or peach. Mango is my favorite of the fruit teas, in case any of you are wondering what I'd like for Christmas.

When the tea party is over, I enjoy watching Leslie clean up and put everything back in order.

I've heard some "experts" say not to use dishwashing detergent in a teapot, but I personally think that's a bunch of bunk. In America, you just don't feel clean unless you've had a bath or a shower, and since I'm serving food, for Heaven's sake, I think it's more than fine when Leslie swirls a few of her Dawn soapsuds around inside me. Mmm. I'm getting that ticklish feeling again just thinking about it.

So remember: teacups may be more well-known for their speaking abilities, but I say, power to the pot. ("The" pot, not "pot," of course. Teapots have standards just like anyone else.)

And the next time you go to a tea party, you might want to be a little more careful with your conversation. You never know who might be listening!

A Year of Teatime Tales

30
Teatime in Paradise

Megan couldn't believe how rested and refreshed she felt. That had to have been the best night's sleep in the history of, well, ever.

She opened the sliding glass door and looked out at the landscape she'd been too preoccupied to check out when she'd first arrived. She'd never seen grass so green, skies so blue, or clouds so magnificently white. She stepped out onto the patio and inhaled deeply. She looked toward the ocean—or what she thought was the ocean. It was too brilliantly aquamarine to be a lake, yet she could see across it to the massive homes on the other side. Maybe it was just some secluded bay. She had so many questions.

Suddenly thirsty, Megan walked inside for a drink and noticed a piece of paper on the sofa. The handwritten note read, "Meet me in the garden across the bridge once you're

up and about. I'm so looking forward to your first teatime here. Love, Abby."

Aunt Abby was already here? Megan hadn't seen her aunt in twenty-something years and wondered what she was like now. Not wanting to waste another second, she slipped out the sliding glass door and headed across the bridge.

Again, Megan inhaled the sweet air and marveled at the fragrance. Gardenias? No. Lilies? Not exactly. What *was* that sweetness in the air? She would have to ask her aunt.

Near the end of the bridge, Megan looked for some sign of which way to go.

"Megan? Is that you?"

Megan looked up and saw her favorite aunt.

"Aunt Abby!" Megan ran to her, and the two embraced. Megan hoped she wouldn't end up crying like a blubbering fool but then realized she no longer wanted to cry.

"I'm so happy you're here," Abby said. "Come sit down, and let's catch up."

Megan had to laugh. There was quite a bit to catch up on! She couldn't help gazing at the stunning table before her. She looked around to see who had set up such a gorgeous scene, but no one appeared. The table and two chairs were made of what looked like fine gold, the tabletop ringed with sparkling gemstones. Again, Megan had the sensation that things were different here.

The teacups and saucers were enchanting, made of a combination of glass and the sheerest, most pearlized porcelain she'd ever seen. Yet Megan couldn't detect a seam. She ran her finger around the exterior of the cup, searching for the spot where the two materials were joined, but found nothing. It wasn't possible for something to be made of both porcelain and glass, was it?

Behind one of the clear glass panels of her teacup, Megan saw a pale brown liquid. "You ordered Darjeeling for me?"

"Not exactly," her aunt said with a smile. "We don't call things by their old names up here. But it's similar to the tea you once enjoyed, yes."

"The tea in this cup is two different colors," Megan observed. "There's a paler brown one right here, on the other side of the teacup."

"That's the mango tea," Abby said. "You always said it was a shame you had to choose a single tea in your teacup, so now you don't have that limitation anymore." Megan looked astonished, but Abby simply grinned. It was always fun to have tea with new arrivals.

The wind whistled softly, and flying in on the breeze was an exquisite four-tiered server. Like the teacups, it was made of porcelain and glass. The sandwiches, savories, sweets, and a mysterious fourth tier of treats were absolute works of art.

The cucumber on the sandwiches—or what looked like cucumber—had been carved into a rose, complete with ruffled petals and even leaves. But cucumbers couldn't be carved so intricately. Megan looked puzzled.

"No, it's not a cucumber," Abby said, amused.

"What is it?"

"Take a bite."

Megan munched the beautiful sandwich and thought she'd died and gone to—

"Mmmm!" she said. "This is so good! It's like a cucumber, but not. It's …"

"It's something you've never had before, but get used to it. You'll be tasting a lot of delicious things, and you'll run out of words to describe them. Fortunately, we have a library up here with books containing words you've never heard before, and you're going to love them."

Megan was startled by the bouncing Boston Terrier licking her ankle. "Darjie! I knew you would be here!"

"Only you would have named a dog after your favorite tea."

Megan laughed as she hugged her beloved terrier, then she heard some voices nearby. She looked up in time to see a man and woman walking by and sharing jokes.

"Aunt Abby! That was—"

"Queen Victoria? Oh, honey, she's just another family member here. That's not even what we call her anymore."

"And she was talking with—"

"Robin Williams, as you knew him? Quite the prankster, that one. If you thought he was funny before …"

Megan shook her head. She couldn't quite comprehend all the surprises of this new place.

"Close your eyes for a moment, Megan."

She did as requested

"Now open them."

Before her sat a beautiful pedestal cake plate bearing the most luscious chocolate dessert Megan had ever seen. "Gold leaf? Seriously?" she asked.

"Actually, we use only pure gold up here. And it's all-you-can-eat, so enjoy!"

Megan laughed, her heart so full she could hardly stand it.

"Aunt Abby?"

"Yes?"

"When do I get to see Him again?"

"Whenever you wish, dear. Would you like to see Him now?"

"Oh yes, Aunt Abby. I've got to tell Him thank you. For, you know …"

Abby stood and held out her hand.

"Yes, dear. I do know, so let's go. And by the way, your tea will still be hot when we get back!"

But as it is written, Eye hath not seen, nor ear heard, neither have entered into the heart of man, the things which God hath prepared for them that love him.—I Corinthians 2:9

31

Planning for the Ladies Guild Fall Tea

"Brenda, why don't you sit down and have some tea sandwiches while you're here?"

"No, thanks, Mary Lou. I have such a tiny little appetite, and if I eat those, I won't be hungry when Cliff takes me to dinner tonight."

"Come on," she says, pushing the plate of tea sandwiches and a small glass bowl of cheese spread toward me. "Just one so I won't feel bad."

"All right. I'll take just one," I say. Mary Lou is known for her pimiento cheese, and the way she slices her sandwiches ribbon-style is just precious, which is one reason I asked her to join the Tea Society where I'm the president.

But I'm not here to eat. I'm here to tell her about the St. Margaret's Episcopal Church Ladies Guild Fall Tea.

"I still don't understand what the Methodists did at their Mother's Day Tea to make you mad," Mary Lou says.

She's one of my dearest friends, but Lord, that woman can frustrate me. I'm so frazzled, I reach for a second pimiento cheese tea sandwich.

"They didn't make me *mad*," I say, then I take a bite of sandwich just so she can see how completely fine I am with everything. "I just realized they were looking for a newcomer to head up their refreshment committee, and you and I both know I'm way overqualified for that."

"Tell me again what happened at the tea?"

I sigh. "I did practically *everything* for that tea, including all the sandwiches, and most of those women didn't lift a finger to help. But you know me, I don't ever say anything. Now Kathy Brown helped, bless her heart, but that woman is a *saint*. I still can't believe she got there at six a.m. just so we'd all have hot scones at teatime."

Mary Lou has supposedly had lunch already, but she opens a big bag of Fritos while I eat one more pimiento cheese tea sandwich. I thought she had signed up for Weight Watchers, but those classes don't appear to be doing her any good.

Mary Lou still doesn't seem to understand the seriousness of what happened at the Mother's Day Tea.

"So the tea went fine?" she asks. Mary Lou was supposed to come but had some kind of family emergency that day. I never did hear any more about that.

"Yes, but after the tea, the pastor's wife didn't even stay and help clean up," I say.

"Pastors' wives aren't janitors, Brenda. Why on earth should she clean up?"

I stick out my tongue at Mary Lou, who is being so ornery today.

"Go on with your story," she says. "So what else made you mad at the Methodists?"

"Nothing made me *mad*, it just hurt my feelings."

"What hurt your feelings, then?"

"When it was time to leave, most of the women told me what a good job I'd done, but the leader of their women's ministry just asked me if I wanted to go on the mission trip to Costa Rica next spring. Can you believe that?"

"What? You don't like missions?"

I roll my eyes and reach for a fork so I can eat that pimiento cheese spread. "Of course I do, but she didn't even thank me for anything. Don't you think she should have? I couldn't believe it. So when Erica Gillingham at St. Margaret's asked if I would be one of the lifestyle experts at their fall tea—"

"Lifestyle expert?" roars Mary Lou, nearly choking on a Frito. "When did you become a 'lifestyle expert'?"

Mary Lou is going to have to start keeping up with the movers and shakers in this town if she plans on us remaining friends. "You know how often I'm asked to speak about my role as president of the Tea Society. Don't you think that qualifies?"

"I guess," Mary Lou says, taking a swig of her sweet tea. "Sounds like you'll enjoy it." Mary Lou drinks out of plastic glasses, not that there's anything wrong with that.

"Anyway," I say, "the point is that the Episcopal ladies want me on the program, I don't have to prepare food, and"—I pause to give Mary Lou the full effect—"I even get an *honorarium*. These ladies know how to treat a professional."

"Uh-huh," Mary Lou says, suddenly fishing around in the bottom of the Fritos bag.

"So how are things with the Baptists?" I ask, just to change the subject. I don't want Mary Lou to think I'm too good to keep up with my old church.

"Fine," she says. "The fall Bible studies are gearing up, and Starla Mooneyham's going to lead a study of the book of Esther."

"*Starla* is going to teach? That's certainly different," I say. What I'm thinking is, *I can't believe Starla Mooneyham is still head of the ladies ministry there. And I still can't believe she turned down my Waldorf Chicken Salad Mini Croissants for the spring tea.*

"You're not still mad at her for not choosing your chicken salad sandwiches for the spring tea, are you?"

"That was actually *Waldorf* Chicken Salad on *Mini Croissants*, but no, I was not then and am not now *mad* about it."

"Okeydokey," says Mary Lou, folding up her Fritos bag. "So when's this shindig at St. Margaret's?"

"September fifth. And I've been asked to display some of my teawares and need you to help me set everything up. Will you?"

"You know I will. That's all this visit was about?"

"Yes. Why?"

Mary Lou shrugs, and I tell her I need to get going.

Slipping my purse over my shoulder, I say, "Trust me, Mary Lou. These Episcopal ladies are going to have the nicest tea this town has ever seen."

"Can't wait," Mary Lou says, but she's rummaging through her cabinets and soon pulls out a box of Little Debbie Swiss Rolls.

"Bye, Mary Lou."

"Bye, Brenda."

I can't wait for September. Besides, it's so nice to have finally found a church home.

32
First Day of School

"Mommy, when Sissy be home?" Braden, my three-year-old, seemed to miss his big sister as much as I did. I found it hard to believe it was the first day of first grade for my oldest child.

It seemed like only yesterday that Dan and I were wondering why I hadn't gotten pregnant after nearly two years of marriage. Fertility testing indicated nothing was preventing us from getting pregnant, we just didn't.

Then, a few months later, I found out I was indeed expecting, and before we knew it, our sweet Abigail was coming home with us in that pretty pink blanket that Dan's mother knitted.

I remember the Minnie Mouse party we had for Abigail's first birthday, and the My Little Pony party when she turned two. She was into Yo Gabba Gabba at three, and we celebrated her fourth birthday while on a family vacation to Disney

World. There was that trip out west to see the grandparents and go horseback riding when she turned five. It all seemed just days ago. Where had the time gone?

"Can I have a popsicle?"

Braden's request jerked me back to reality. I reached into the freezer and wondered if Abigail had had lunch yet. It was almost noon, but some of the moms I knew had told me horror stories of their kids eating lunch as early as nine thirty in the morning. What if Abigail was hungry? What if I'd given her too much juice for breakfast and she had to go to the bathroom and couldn't make it in time? Those kinds of things happened, I knew.

Gwen down the street got called to the office on the first day of school last year when her Emily had an accident. I wasn't sure who was more embarrassed, mother or daughter, but I worried about something like that happening to Abigail.

I looked at my cell phone, but no, there were no messages. And it was fully charged, so I was ready for a call if one came.

I'd already finished my first cup of tea that morning but suddenly realized my teacup was missing. Had I taken it into the living room? I checked, but there was no sign of it.

Maybe it was in the laundry room where I'd gone to double-check my PTA meeting calendar that hung there. No. My cup wasn't in there either. Odd. But then everything about that day had felt slightly odd.

I knew I wasn't the first mom to send her child off to school, and I wouldn't be the last, but no one had warned me how hard it would be. After caring for my child's every need for almost six years, I suddenly was entrusting her safety to someone else?

Thank goodness there was a prayer group at church for first-day-of-school moms. I was so grateful when I got a text from Wendy, whose kids are in middle school this year. It said, "Praying 4 U 2Day!" I sure hoped Wendy kept it up.

And I sure hoped Abigail was having a good day. I had been determined to make her first day of school special, so Dan and I had surprised her by placing a small vase of yellow flowers on her nightstand soon after we got up, making sure it was the first thing she would see when her Hello Kitty alarm clock went off.

The funny thing was that Abigail seemed much less worried about the first day of school than I was. When I walked her into her classroom and left her there, I found myself tearing up, but she was fine. "Bye, Mommy," she said, giving me a peck on the cheek and heading in to get a sticker from Miss Lauren, her teacher.

"She'll be fine," Miss Lauren had told me. "I promise."

Miss Lauren looked as though she had just graduated two weeks ago, but she seemed smart, sweet, and cheerful, which was pretty much all I wanted in my child's teacher. I wondered if Miss Lauren would think Abigail was gifted.

As I pondered all that, I reached for the teacup that I usually kept next to my seat on the sectional in the living room, but it wasn't there. What had I done with that teacup?

Suddenly aware that I hadn't heard Braden in a while, I passed through the living room and headed down the hall to his room. No Braden.

I checked in my and Dan's room. Nothing.

It dawned on me to look in Abigail's room. Braden was sitting on the floor in front of her nightstand, and he held up his chubby little hands and shoved my missing teacup before me.

"For you, Mommy. Frow-ers," he said.

Oh no.

He had stripped down Abigail's beautiful first-day-of-school bouquet and plopped the tattered little yellow flowers into my teacup.

"Oh, wow," I said, trying to recover as gracefully as I could. "You made this just for me?"

"Uh-huh," he said, a proud smile on his face.

What could I do?

"Thank you, sweetheart," I said, scooping him up into a big hug. "I love it. And most of all, I love you!"

There would be other flowers. In fact, I would run by the grocery store on the way to pick up Abigail and get a replacement bouquet. If I knew my child, she would be so eager to tell me about everything that had happened at school, she wouldn't even think to look at those flowers for hours—if then.

After all, just a few short years and I would be sitting at home one day wondering how Braden's first day of school was going.

Meanwhile, it was time to find another teacup and have that second cup of tea.

A Year of Teatime Tales

33
The Whisper

People never know precisely where and when I'll show up, and I work hard at keeping it that way. Sometimes I'm impulsive and make my first visit in July, but then again, I'm just as likely to show up in the dog days of August, or even early September, teasing my admirers with the promise of what will soon be there to stay.

I'm a seasonal visitor to most places around the world, and I can only say that—and I hope this doesn't sound too prideful—there are very few people who don't eagerly await my arrival.

It's certainly nice to be loved, and why shouldn't I be? I bring word that so many wonderful things are on the way. The wonderful things don't appear on the exact day I arrive—for my visit is always just a fleeting one—but they do arrive not long afterward. Hayrides and apple festivals. College football games. Elementary school bake sales. Halloween and Thanksgiving. Late nights of stargazing around the fire pit.

The atmosphere not only *feels* different once I've made my visit, it even *smells* different. Soon, like clockwork, everyone's having Cranberry Autumn tea—a personal favorite—and hot apple cider. Bakers start turning out plump loaves of pumpkin bread and their best pecan pies. Barbecue smoke wafts over the backyard fence just in time to signal a last-minute invite luring the neighbors to supper. And oh, the caramel popcorn and cotton candy at the county fair. That rich, delicious hot sugar smell alone is a feast for the senses. And those things can't be found in January, April, or June. Only after I show up.

What I absolutely adore is that shortly after my arrival, everyone begins to chill out—literally and figuratively. Cooler temperatures move in, and so does a more relaxed, less frenzied pace. Whatever a man or woman's leisure pursuit, they enjoy it more once I've worked my magic. Gardeners, suddenly shed of summer's heat, head back outside to play in the dirt again. Fishermen and fisherwomen know that lakes will be low but spirits high since the bass will be coming out of their summer slump.

And I admit I have a soft spot for quilters. Yes, I know they ply their needles year-round, but after I give the go-ahead, they seem to go into overdrive. Inspired by the brilliant coloring of the trees, the quilters gather their honeyed golds, flaming reds, bright browns, and opulent oranges in an effort to mimick what's going on in nature outside their homes.

Soon, they'll be at their sewing machines and wooden embroidery hoops, diligently working on quilts in the Log Cabin, Baltimore Album, or Wedding Ring pattern. Perhaps even a few Maple Leaf quilts will come to life in their hands. I hear about their creations every single year, and every single year, I love to give the quilters—and the gardeners, and the fishermen and fisherwomen—encouragement to indulge in the leisure pursuits that bring them so much pleasure.

Knowing how important a role I play, I do give a great deal of thought to the time of my arrival. It can't be so soon that my message seems ridiculous, and it can't be so late that they don't have a few weeks' fun of looking forward. The timing of my visit is critical, whether they realize it or not.

Also, there's the fact that I don't—can't, really—choose to show up everywhere on the same day. That would be tiring. Plus, even I can't be in two different places at one time, even though some people mistakenly think I can.

Then there are those who disregard my existence entirely and stubbornly insist on consulting their calendar to determine when I'll show up. As if a piece of paper—or today, some silly electronic device—could possibly predict when I'll be there. I still get a kick out of the folly of using a manmade tool to predict something so magical.

So, I am often asked, where did you come from? People are forever intrigued by the mystery surrounding me. I was born thousands of years ago, created in a whoosh and a whirl. There's not an easy way to explain it, but for those who ask, I simply say that my mother was the wind and my father was the air. That usually does the trick without revealing too much of my mystique.

While I can't be contained within the pages of a calendar, I can be found, and found easily, by those whose senses have been trained to find me. They see me in the flutter of the first fallen leaf, and they feel me in that quiet moment when the last of summer's heat pauses, for just a single second, to permit a slight, oh-so-slight breeze.

And then I politely disappear for just a little longer, because I am, of course, the whisper of fall.

34
Those Tea Party Pinkies

I couldn't wait for Social Studies to end. Just my luck that I had gotten Ms. Bradley for the year. Dang, that woman droned on and on. She last updated her wardrobe in, like, the nineties or something, and she had that big long chin hair that she wouldn't pluck for some reason. Hannah said that one day, she was going to bring tweezers to class and just go up there and yank that thing out, but I told her that was crazy. The school resource officer would probably arrest Hannah for assault or something, and there I'd be, having to visit my best friend in juvie.

To earn extra credit for the year, Hannah and I signed up for community service projects and volunteered to work with the historical society like we did last year. I had figured it would just be a bunch of boring old people sitting around talking about the Civil War, but it wasn't like that at all—not unless somebody just *wanted* to talk about the Civil War.

That was also how I met Claire Wilson, their party person. Her official title was something like "Community Outreach Coordinator," but I worked with her last summer and got the scoop. I found out she loved to party, and she wanted to invite me to all their parties—or "community outreach" events—but she said they always had a lot of booze flowing, and it freaked out the grown-ups to have teenagers around. Like we didn't know they liked their beer and wine. Duh.

But that afternoon, Miss Claire wanted me and Hannah to help with an afternoon tea for some girls in the after-school program at one of the elementary schools. Hannah told Ms. Bradley we needed to leave class early to help with the tea. She explained that we would be teaching the girls about Victorian tea etiquette. Brianna Simpson heard that and started saying "Fiddle dee dee" over and over, like we were going to *Gone With the Wind* tryouts. Idiot. She probably didn't even know that the Victorian period lasted until 1901, and she probably thought Queen Victoria was a rapper. But I didn't want to waste time thinking about stupid old Brianna Simpson.

Hannah said Brianna was jealous because Joshua Taylor sat by me at lunch today. I told Hannah that was ridiculous. Joshua had lived down the street from me all my life, and our parents were best friends. I hoped he didn't get mixed up with a skank like Brianna, but I wouldn't judge him even if he did. If he wanted to go with someone like her, why should I care?

When Hannah and I got to the historical society, the first thing we did was get dressed in some hoopskirts and gowns that Miss Claire had ready for us. I got the pink one, and Hannah wore the blue one. We wore big old gaudy hats too. Little girls loved those.

Ten girls were at the tea party, and we decided Hannah would go first and give them a few etiquette tips. Since Hannah had two older sisters and never got to be the boss, I didn't mind if she got more speaking time than I did. I just had one bratty little brother, and I generally got along with him, except when he kept adding new games to my iPad without asking.

As Miss Claire and the other volunteers brought out the tea trays, Hannah told the girls they were supposed to eat sandwiches first, then scones, then sweets. One little girl was already nibbling on a chocolate-covered strawberry, but Hannah and I just grinned at each other. We knew it was bad etiquette to make your guests feel bad when they messed up.

When it was my turn, I told the girls not to hold their teacups with their pinkies up. Somebody was always telling little girls to drink tea with their pinkies up, and it drove me crazy. Why did people do that? One little girl said that was a relief because her pinkie was already tired.

Once the tea was over, I texted my mom to come pick us up, and Hannah and I changed into jeans and T-shirts. As we dressed in the bathroom, someone knocked. It was Miss Claire asking us to stop by her office before we left.

When we got there, Miss Claire had two navy-blue gift bags on her desk.

"These are for you, Megan and Hannah," she said, handing one to Hannah and one to me. "Just a small thank-you for helping with the kids in the after-school program this afternoon. You girls are such a big help around here."

Hannah and I were beaming. It was nice to be appreciated.

My cell phone pinged to let me know I had a text. It was my mom telling me she'd pulled up out front.

"Mom's here, so we've gotta run. Thank you," I said, holding up my bag as I left.

"Yeah, thanks, Miss Claire," Hannah said.

We dropped Hannah off at her mom's gift shop downtown, and then Mom dropped me by the house before going to buy groceries. I'd had a few cucumber sandwiches and some Earl Grey at the tea party, but I was still hungry. While I warmed up leftover pizza, I opened my gift.

Underneath the layers of dark blue tissue was a white box. I wasn't surprised to open the box and see a cool teacup and saucer inside. Lavender was my favorite color, and the teacup had pink and lavender flowers on it.

My mom was a big tea drinker, so I got one of her tea bags and made a cup of Darjeeling to go with my pizza.

Stupid old Brianna Simpson probably didn't even know how to hold a teacup. And if she ever asked me about it, I was definitely going to tell her how important it was to always hold her pinkie up. Always. Ha!

35
A Nutty Dessert

Ruth reached down into the kitchen cabinet for the tin loaf pan, its scratched and darkened metal testifying to years of use. The loaf pan was just where it always was, right-hand side of the shelf, on top of the muffin tins and cookie sheets. As she pulled it out, she paused to massage her hip. Her doctor kept telling her she needed to have a hip replacement soon, but she was content to pop a few Advil and try to live with the pain a little longer.

Fortunately, she didn't have to reach or stoop to gather the flour, sugar, and other staples she needed for baking. That set of brown Tupperware canisters was one of the best purchases she had ever made. The lids on those canisters still fit tight as a tick, just as sturdy as the day she bought them, and besides, they matched the rooster print of the kitchen wallpaper.

Walking slowly over to her small but tidy pantry, Ruth looked on the second shelf and pulled out a jar of Jippy Peanut Butter. Ruth had eaten nothing but Jippy since it first came out in the fifties. It was the only peanut butter her kids would eat, and the "kids" were almost senior citizens. Her son loved the Creamy, but her daughter wouldn't eat anything but Extra Crunchy. Ruth kept jars of each on hand at all times, just in case the kids stopped by.

After she finished sifting and measuring her dry ingredients, she added the peanut butter, eggs, and milk. She greased the pan, poured the batter inside, sprinkled some chopped peanuts on top—after munching a few—and set the timer for one hour. Soon, the rich scent of hot peanuts filled the air.

Peanut butter had long been a staple in her home. Her late husband, Bill, had always had a tablespoon of peanut butter—the Creamy—on his toast each morning. Occasionally, Ruth joined him in that, but she preferred the Extra Crunchy. Over the years, she'd made just about every peanut butter dessert imaginable: peanut butter cookies, peanut butter bars, peanut butter balls at Christmas. Her chocolate peanut butter pie was always a big hit when she took it to the Senior Center's monthly birthday parties.

That evening, Ruth's neighbor Eloise was coming over for dessert and tea, so Ruth was baking a favorite treat, her Peanut Butter Tea Loaf.

Eloise, who was hard of hearing, loved it, but Ruth had had a devil of a time explaining why it was called a "tea" loaf.

"Is there tea in there?" Eloise had asked, hollering as if she thought Ruth was hard of hearing too.

"No, no tea," Ruth had said.

"I know it's *nutty*. I said, is there *tea* in there?" Eloise had asked, louder.

Ruth had explained that a tea loaf was just a name and didn't really mean that much. A true Anglophile, she knew that "tea loaf" usually referred to those English cakes made with dried fruits and served in slices with butter on them, but she didn't have the patience to try to explain that to Eloise.

Once, Ruth had made the mistake of trying to watch one of her entertainment programs while Eloise was there.

"Who are all those gals?" Eloise had asked.

"They're the Kardashians," Ruth replied.

"Car dash what? That's a funny name. And why do they all wear so much makeup?"

Ruth finally learned to keep the TV off when Eloise visited.

When the timer sounded, Ruth removed the tea loaf from the oven and let it rest in the pan on a wire rack for ten minutes. When Bill was still alive, he'd always gotten into the baked goods before they cooled, and she'd slapped his hands away many times. She smiled at the memory. If only Bill's hands were there to reach for a fresh-out-of-the-oven dessert once more.

The rooster teakettle on the stovetop was starting to whistle, so Ruth went ahead and prepared her cup of tea. She liked a strong English Breakfast blend at any time of day, and Eloise didn't have a preference one way or the other. She came for the gossip more than anything.

At seven o'clock, Ruth heard a knock at the door and knew it was her friend.

She looked through the peephole and saw some familiar gray hair. "Come in," Ruth said. "Let's just sit in the kitchen and have dessert."

"You're gonna miss your program with all those car dash women on it," Eloise said. "You don't mind?"

"Not a bit," Ruth said.

She prepared Eloise's tea and brought it to the table along with a pink glass plate bearing the sliced tea loaf.

"Is this that peanut butter thing I like?"

"It sure is," Ruth said.

"It's got tea in it, right?"

"No, no tea."

"I know it's *nutty*. You always say that, but I said *does it have tea* in it?"

"No, it does not have tea in it," Ruth said, speaking each word loudly and clearly. Maybe she needed to rethink having Eloise over so often.

"I was kinda wantin' to watch that entertainment program over here since my TV's on the blink," Eloise said. "Do you mind?"

Ruth shuffled back to the pantry and gathered two lightweight TV trays to set up in the den to hold their food. She turned on the TV just as a familiar young face appeared on the screen.

"Do you like that Molly Silas?" Eloise said. "I don't much care for her."

Ruth grinned. "I need a refill. How 'bout you?"

Eloise, her eyes glued to the screen, nodded and handed over her teacup.

Ruth was still in the kitchen when Eloise called out, "Hey, did you hear about Bruce Jenner?"

"Give me strength, Lord," Ruth said. And just for good measure, she reached in the can for a few peanuts before rejoining her friend. It was, after all, much better to eat nuts than to be nuts.

A Year of Teatime Tales

36
I Will Always Love You

Paula couldn't wait to hit the Labor Day weekend flea markets. In her town, sellers set up everywhere they could squeeze a card table or canvas tent, from Main Street to the nearby neighborhoods, and she saved her tips all summer so she'd have plenty of ones, fives, and tens to spend the first weekend in September.

She was a waitress at Hank's Hog Heaven Barbecue Palace, and the place would be doing a booming business all weekend, but Paula always took Friday and Saturday mornings off on Labor Day weekend to shop the flea markets. The barbecue buffs would get along just fine until she arrived later.

That Saturday morning, Paula hopped out of bed at six and tried not to wake Dennis, her husband, or Moon Pie and RC, the tabby cats she'd rescued from the dumpster behind Hank's a few years back. Dennis had pitched a fit when she came home with them, mainly because she always got too attached to her pets, and they always died. Fortunately, Moon

Pie and RC seemed to be in great health. Neither Dennis nor the cats stirred as Paula padded to the bathroom, dressed in comfy jeans and a Luke Bryan T-shirt, and pulled on her favorite cowboy boots.

She put a pot of coffee on for Dennis and filled her thermos with unsweet tea from the fridge. Paula drank unsweet tea constantly at Hank's. Slinging barbecue was hard work, and she got thirsty as soon as she hit the floor each day.

Carrying her thermos in one hand, Paula used the other to reach for her handbag. Her friends had wondered how a waitress could afford a Dooney & Bourke ostrich hobo bag, and she'd been happy to tell them about the night a customer dropped a two-hundred-dollar tip. She'd gone to the mall the very next morning and bought the purse. It was six months before Dennis noticed it. When he'd asked if it was new, she told him, honestly, that it was not.

She looked on the kitchen counter and was pleased Dennis had left the keys to his Ford F-150 as she'd asked him to. She wasn't looking to buy furniture, but she never knew what she might find and wanted to be prepared.

Once in the truck, Paula poured some tea into a Tervis tumbler. For the millionth time, she thought how much she loved her tea. After cranking the truck and turning on country radio, Paula pulled onto the highway. Soon, she was sipping tea to Billy Currington's "Good Directions," tapping the gas pedal as he sang of asking "Miss Belle" for some of her sweet tea.

The colorful flea market tents were up on Main Street as Paula passed through downtown, then slipped into a parking space and prepared to shop. First stop was the Kiwanis funnel cake booth.

"Funny to be serving *you* for a change," said Bill McHenry, the new Kiwanis president, as he handed over her funnel cake sprinkled with powdered sugar.

"Yeah, and I kinda like it," Paula joked, handing over a twenty and telling Bill to keep the change. Kiwanis did so much good in their community, she liked to give a little extra when she could.

Paula said hello to some of the regulars from Hank's, then

moseyed on to the other booths. Within fifteen minutes, she'd purchased some silver cowboy boot earrings, a candle that looked like an apple pie, and a throw rug crocheted from old T-shirts. Paula thought the colorful rug would look great in her bathroom.

There didn't seem to be as many junkers as usual. Paula saw her old high school friend, Beverly, who liked antiques and "upcycled" treasures, as they called them these days.

"Listen, if you want some bargains, head over to Wilson Avenue," Beverly said. "There's a neighborhood sale, and they're letting stuff go cheap. I got two rockers, a dresser, three quilts, and a butter churn for under a hundred bucks."

Paula thanked her for the tip and headed to the truck. She polished off her funnel cake, trashed the paper plate, and was ready to roll.

Wilson Avenue was just three blocks away, and Paula couldn't wait to get there. She loved old stuff. In fact, she'd recently redecorated her living room in the Victorian style. That had surprised Dennis, who always thought Paula was fine with his camouflage recliner and pit group. When he came home one day to find a burgundy floral sofa and love seat in their place, he realized big changes were afoot.

"Mornin'," Paula said to the woman in charge of the sale. It never hurt to be friendly. Sometimes, it got you a better deal.

Cars were pulling in quickly, but Paula spotted the antique silverplate set before the other shoppers did. She'd seen something similar in a magazine, but old silver cost a fortune. The set was just ten dollars for three pieces. She wasn't even sure what they were. A sugar, creamer, and maybe some kind of fancy serving piece?

Paula took the silver to the checkout table and continued looking. She found a tapestry pillow for the living room for three dollars and a matching footstool for five. She was about to bypass the china and glassware when she realized the little wooden cart they sat on was for sale. Ten bucks? Heck yeah!

Paula found a rusty toolbox she knew Dennis would love for ten dollars, and for free, she got a brand-new scratch toy for Moon Pie and RC. The seller just wanted rid of it. Paula was happy to help.

After paying up, Paula got in the truck, refilled her tea tumbler, and cranked up the radio. A favorite song was starting to play, Dolly Parton's "I Will Always Love You."

As she cruised through town and headed home, Paula held up her tea tumbler and suddenly laughed. "Yes, my friend, I will *always* love you!" And she sipped her tea with a smile.

37

Plain, Reliable Betty

Dr. Cohen's counseling office wasn't what I'd expected. I had been nervous about going there ever since I made the appointment. What if all she did was nod her head and peer over her reading glasses and say, "Hmm, I see." What if she was mean to me? Worst of all, what if she'd never seen anyone so needy and couldn't help me? Still, I knew I needed to do something, so I made the appointment, and there I was.

Right away, I found the office pleasantly inviting. I'd expected gray furnishings and walls, perhaps a few motivational posters with perky sayings on them. Instead, the beautiful reception area with sage green walls and fern-patterned sofas didn't feel like a counseling office at all. It felt more like a cozy living room.

After I checked in, I sat down and picked up a copy of *People* magazine, pleased to find it was current. Most doctors' offices seemed to prefer dog-eared copies about a decade old.

"Betty Brown? Dr. Cohen will see you now."

I took a deep breath and placed the *People* magazine back on the table. I would just have to wait to find out which Hollywood power couple was divorcing that week.

Like the reception area, the doctor's office was a nice surprise. First, I was relieved that there was no red leather couch for me to lie down on. Instead, two beautiful wingback chairs in a turquoise geometric print sat before the doctor's desk, a simple glass and metal piece. For some reason, I liked that her desk was glass. Talk about transparency!

Dr. Cohen, who had short, spiky gray hair, stood and shook my hand. "I'm so happy to meet you, Betty. Before we begin, would you mind telling me a little about yourself?"

That was what I was there for, after all, so I gave her the scoop.

"I was born in England, and my family moved to this country in the 1960s. I went through elementary, middle, and high school just fine with no rebellion, little of the customary teenage angst. My parents said I gave them very little trouble."

I paused, and Dr. Cohen nodded affirmingly. I liked that.

"So the early years were fine, but in college…" I said with a sniffle. "That's when it first hit me how truly plain I was. Or *am*, rather. All the other gals had dates every weekend, but I never got asked out. Not once. Oh, I did things with groups of friends, but it wasn't the same. I always wanted a boyfriend, but I never got one."

When I paused, Dr. Cohen gently asked, "And you're still single today?"

"Yes," I said, and the tears began to trickle once more. "I'm still just *plain, reliable Betty*, the one everyone relies on but no one ever thinks to talk to at a party. I'm so taken for granted. Dr. Cohen, is something wrong with me?"

Dr. Cohen smiled and shook her head.

"Betty, in both my personal and professional opinion, there's certainly nothing wrong with wanting to belong, with wanting a relationship. But what I'm concerned about is that you seem to be letting others define you."

Puzzled by what she'd said, I stopped sniffling.

"How so?"

"First, do you call yourself *plain, reliable Betty?*" she asked.

"Well, no."

"So you've heard someone else call you that?"

"No one's ever actually called me *plain* to my face, but I can tell they're thinking it. And they have called me *reliable*. Everybody says that like it's so great."

"So you would prefer to be thought *un*reliable?"

"No!" I quickly said. "Of course not."

Dr. Cohen was hard to read right then. She said, "So why would you mind being thought of as reliable?"

"Hmm." I hesitated. "I guess I don't mind being thought of as reliable, but I don't want to be thought of *only* as reliable. Does that make sense?"

"Betty, in my practice, I see teapots every day who are thoroughly unreliable. Some of them have cracks and chips that won't ever be repaired. Some of the so-called pretty ones are such narcissists, all they do is sit around staring at their own reflection in the china cabinet. They've never actually been called into service and have certainly never proven to be reliable serving pieces."

I had not given much thought to those attractive teapots I had envied. "Really?" I said.

"You would be surprised at the teapots that have come into this office. And then there are those who truly want to serve but have some unfortunate physical defect that makes them unable to function well."

"I know just who you're talking about—the drippers!" I said. "I don't mean to brag, doctor, but I never drip. Ever."

"I know that, Betty. Your family is well known for your excellent service through the years. You've always been considered ... well, plain and reliable, if you don't mind my saying so."

I found myself sitting up a little straighter in that pretty wingback chair of hers. "I think I see your point," I said.

"Why don't you go home and work on a list of all the things that are actually good about being plain and reliable," Dr. Cohen said, "and then come back in two weeks, and we'll discuss how you feel about it."

I nodded, told her I'd book the appointment on my way out, and thanked her for her time. Dr. Cohen had certainly given me a new way of looking at things.

As I stood at the reception desk, waiting to get my appointment card, I noticed a handsome gentleman, a hunter green Chatsford teapot, waiting in a chair and holding the new issue of *Sports Illustrated*.

And to my surprise and amazement, he smiled at me! Was I plain and reliable? Yes. And so much more.

38
Art and Inspiration

Teresa's mother had given her that first teacup, a simple Blue Willow cup and saucer. When her grandmother passed away, Teresa inherited a pretty cobalt-blue cup and saucer by Royal Albert. A girlfriend who often sat in her kitchen sipping tea noticed the blue teawares and began to give her blue teacups for Christmas and birthdays. And so a collection began.

While Teresa enjoyed drinking tea from the pretty teacups, she got the greatest pleasure from admiring their beautiful colors and patterns. She marveled that such miniscule pieces of art appeared on such thoroughly useful vessels.

Teresa was taking art classes at the local rec department, and she'd made excellent progress with her watercolor painting. Her instructor had encouraged her to enter a local juried art show, but Teresa didn't feel she was ready for that.

One sunny fall afternoon, Teresa decided to go outside on her patio to paint. First, she focused on the last of the morning glories in the backyard flower garden. The periwinkle color was glorious, and Teresa painted several blossoms, but the result was lackluster. She turned her attention to an autumnal display of white and orange pumpkins. A fall-themed piece of art would be nice to have in her home, but Teresa painted the pumpkins and found them unbearably boring.

She walked into the house to make a cup of cranberry tea. Out of habit, she reached for the Blue Willow teacup from her mother. Teresa caressed it and fingered the rim. It still had that small nick in the back, but if she painted the teacup, who would ever know?

Forgetting the cranberry tea, Teresa headed outside with the Blue Willow teacup and began to compose a scene. Something bothered her, though. The single teacup looked a little too perfect, a little too stiff. She went inside, retrieved three more blue teacups, and headed back outside.

Teresa stacked them haphazardly, staggering the handles and giving the teacups a casual appearance. Bright blue watercolor paints began to fill the paper, and soon, Teresa was quite pleased. Despite the inspiration of nature around her, Teresa had found beauty right in the middle of her kitchen with everyday objects she used and had taken for granted.

For once feeling satisfied with her work, Teresa took the teacup painting to her next art class to share. The instructor, Harriet, asked to speak with her after class.

"Thanks for staying, Teresa. I'm quite impressed with this painting. What do you plan to do with it?"

"I haven't planned to do anything with it," Teresa said. "Hang it in my kitchen, I suppose."

"Are you very attached to it?"

"I like it, obviously, but ... do you have something in mind?"

"I do, actually. Have you heard about the new women's shelter in town?"

"I saw a little about it on Facebook."

"They're holding a fund-raising tea next week, and I'm gathering donations of local art for the silent auction. I would love to have this piece if you'd consider donating it. I'd be very surprised if this didn't bring more attention to your work and perhaps get you a few commissions as well."

"I don't know about all that, but sure, I'll help. What if it doesn't sell, though? I wouldn't want my painting to fall flat in the silent auction."

"You let me worry about that," Harriet said, smiling. "And of course I want you as my guest at the luncheon on September twenty-fourth. Are you free?"

"Yes," Teresa said, "but again, I hope someone likes the painting as much as you do."

"Great. I'm listing an opening bid of one hundred twenty-five dollars, but I bet it'll go for much more."

Teresa gulped. She had never sold a painting in her life. One hundred twenty-five dollars for a watercolor by an unknown artist? Would a bidder ever pay that?

The day of the luncheon, Teresa arrived and was pleased to find a few of her friends were there as well. She sat with Harriet. After the shelter's director welcomed everyone and tea sandwiches were served, the first silent auction item went up. The beautiful oil painting, a fall landscape, was an instant hit, and bidding shot up to three hundred dollars. Teresa began to get nervous. They had announced the name of the artist, so if her own name was announced when her piece went up, she would be embarrassed if there were no bids.

After the scone course, some flower arrangements were auctioned off, followed by another oil painting that sold for six hundred dollars. Teresa began to wonder if her painting had even made the lineup, but following the sweets course, a shelter volunteer brought out the teacup painting and paraded it around the room.

Finally, the auctioneer held up her painting. "May I have an opening bid of one hundred twenty-five dollars?"

A hand went up. The bidding quickly shot up to two hundred, two fifty, three hundred, then three fifty. Before she knew it, Teresa had watched her painting sell for eight hundred dollars. She sat speechless, tears filling her eyes.

"I told you!" Harriet said smugly. "I had a hunch this would be the hit of the auction, and I also think you need to seriously consider painting more works in this style."

"I'm thrilled it did so well, and yes, I'll absolutely think about painting more works like this," Teresa said.

And she did. She went home and thought about how much joy the actual painting of that piece had brought her. Maybe she would create a few others and see if she could place them in local galleries. Maybe she'd create some notecards and prints for sale too. Suddenly, her artistic possibilities seemed endless.

But first, Teresa sat in her kitchen, where she sipped a cup of cranberry tea, looked at her Blue Willow teacup, and again admired its beauty, so pleased she had helped others see it as well.

39
A Prize-Winning Quilt

Myrtle Mae McDaniel was determined to win a blue ribbon at the county fair that fall. She'd placed with every quilt she'd ever entered in the fair, but she was tired of red ribbons and white ribbons and honorable mention ribbons. It was high time she won the blue.

With the war going on, she was surprised there were enough men left in town to even get the fair up and running, but thanks to the persistence of the Taylorsville Women's Club, the fair would go on as usual. The amusement company would arrive at the last of September, just as it always did, but instead of every men's club in town running all the booths and exhibits, the women would be in charge. Before Charles had gone off to war, she usually ended up helping with many of his county fair duties anyway, so she felt very comfortable in that regard. She sure did miss Charles. She missed her brothers, Lou and Lee, too, but in a different kind of way.

"So Myrtle Mae, which quilt are you going to enter this year?" Charlotte Perkins had asked a few weeks ago. Charlotte was one of Myrtle Mae's neighbors—and some of her prime competition in the quilt contest at the county fair. In fact, Charlotte had won blue ribbons the past three years, a fact she did not hesitate to mention if the topic of quilting came up in conversation. And when Charlotte was around, somehow, it often did.

"I haven't decided yet," Myrtle Mae said. "I've finished a half dozen new ones this past year, so I imagine it'll be one of those."

"The judges seemed to like star design quilts last year," Charlotte said. "In fact, now that I think about it, I believe I got a blue ribbon for my Feathered Star quilt at last year's fair."

"That was truly a gorgeous quilt," Myrtle Mae said. She didn't deny that Charlotte was a fine quilter; she just wished Charlotte weren't so inclined to toot her own horn.

Myrtle Mae didn't see any need to tell Charlotte, but she was pretty sure she was going to finish her new appliqued teapot quilt made from flour sacks, and that would be the one she entered in the fair. Like a lot of women who sewed during the war, Myrtle Mae used flour sacks to conserve the "good" material for other uses, and the challenge was to use the colorful, cheerful flour sack prints in new and interesting ways. Myrtle Mae had seen flour sack appliques of baskets, flowers, and stars, but she'd never seen one made with teapots.

She'd looked through her quilt books for a teapot pattern but couldn't find one. Finally, one night after she put Raymond, Harold, and Gloria to bed, she looked at the small cream-colored teapot on her kitchen counter and drew a freehand version of the pot onto a paper grocery sack. When she cut out the template and transferred the design to fabric with a pencil, she was fairly certain she'd discovered a new quilt pattern she would enjoy stitching.

Like her mother, who was from England, Myrtle Mae had grown up drinking brisk black tea rather than coffee. Some of the women in her coffee klatch thought that was just plain odd. Too bad for them and more tea for her, that was Myrtle Mae's philosophy.

Most evenings, she prepared herself a nice hot cup of tea while she worked on the teapot quilt. Myrtle Mae enjoyed selecting the most colorful of the flour sack fabrics to add to her quilt. As she stitched each teapot into place, she whiled away the hours, thinking and praying. She thought about her young family, and she prayed for her husband, brothers, and all of those serving overseas, praying the war would soon come to an end so they could all be together again.

As the teapot quilt came to life, Myrtle Mae found her worries and cares slowly slipping away, just as if they had been absorbed by the pretty cotton prints at her fingertips. Before she knew it, she'd created one hundred of those blocks and began stitching them into ten rows of ten each. The effect, she had to admit, was rather striking. She hoped the quilt judges at the county fair would agree with her.

When the fair opened and all the quilts were judged, Myrtle Mae eagerly entered the quilt exhibit building and was thrilled to see that her teapot quilt had earned the coveted blue ribbon. To her astonishment, the quilt had also received the Best in Show Award, and the judges' comments made her beam with pride: "To Myrtle Mae McDaniel, in recognition of beauty, creativity, and workmanship, and also for patriotism in the creative use of flour sack fabrics, wisely conserving material at this important time in our nation's history."

The other quilters had flocked around Myrtle Mae and congratulated her on the award. Even Charlotte offered congratulations, although she had added, "You know, I almost entered an applique quilt this year, but I went with another star quilt instead. You just never can tell what will strike the judges' fancy each year, can you?"

Before leaving the exhibit building and going in search of her children—who were no doubt riding something that would make them dizzy and eating something that would give them a stomachache—Myrtle Mae looked at the teapot quilt, remembered the thoughts and prayers that had gone into all those stitches, and wondered when Charles and her brothers would get to come home.

A blue ribbon was nice to have, but seeing all her family safely home again? That was the best prize she could ever imagine.

40
A Cup of Hope

It was the lump that every woman dreaded finding. Gail was doing her monthly breast self-exam one morning when she felt the small, hard spot, something so small she was convinced it couldn't possibly be cancer. Still, all her friends who'd had breast cancer insisted that early detection saved lives, and Gail knew better than to let the spot go unchecked. She was sure it would be nothing, so she called her doctor and scheduled an appointment.

It wasn't nothing. It was something. Along with the shock of learning she had cancer came the shock of learning she would need to have a lumpectomy followed by radiation.

Gail loved to quote the popular saying "Ain't nobody got time for that," but she quickly saw that she would have to *make* time for that. Because she hadn't worked outside the home since her children, now in their late twenties, were little, she knew she had it much easier than those women who worked full-time outside the home. And single women. And poor women.

But Gail loved being a volunteer in her community—with Friends of the Library, with Meals on Wheels—and it bothered her that those activities would have to be put on hold for a while.

Her friend Bonnie, a breast cancer survivor herself, said, "Gail, aren't you mad that you got cancer?"

Gail told her that, in all honesty, she was not. Annoyed? Yes. Frightened? She'd have been lying if she said she wasn't. But mad? What would be the point? Lots of people got cancer, Gail told Bonnie, and until they found a cure for the horrible disease, she knew people were going to get it. She considered herself fortunate that her cancer was spotted early, and the doctor had given her the reassuring news that her chance of a full recovery was excellent.

Week two of radiation was going pretty well. Gail had even written about her treatment on Facebook, asking all her friends—the real ones and the ones she hadn't laid eyes on in thirty years—to keep her in their thoughts and prayers.

Her neighbor Pam had been a big help, even preparing dinner for Gail and her husband, Wayne, one night. Wayne was no cook, but he would have happily picked up dinner every night of the week if Gail had asked him to. She enjoyed cooking, but the daily trips for radiation seemed to suck the life out of her.

So Gail was especially happy when she got home from a round of radiation late one afternoon and had a text from Pam. "Call me when you get home. Got a drop-off."

The "drop-off" was a freshly made salad, a pan of Pam's famous mac 'n cheese, a roasted chicken, and some of her fresh-from-the-garden green beans. For dessert, she included a half dozen red velvet cupcakes with cream cheese icing and raspberries on top.

Gail had never realized a gift of food could make her so happy.

It had rained almost every day for two weeks, and today, after Wayne drove her home from radiation, she took a nap. When she woke up, she decided to have the last of those red velvet cupcakes with her afternoon cup of Earl Grey. Instead of using her customary brown pottery mug, though, Gail chose to have tea using one of her aunt's Royal Winton Welbeck teacups. Her aunt had always loved that cheerful yellow pattern, and truthfully, Gail did too. It made her happy just to look at the pretty yellow colors.

Once her tea steeped, she inhaled the strong, fragrant aroma. Earl Grey always perked her up, and today, the tea was quite a needed pick-me-up.

Gail was genuinely trying to eat the healthiest food she could get her hands on—organic juices and fruits and vegetables, for starters—but she wasn't about to let one of Pam's red velvet cupcakes go to waste. After grabbing a napkin from the kitchen, she headed to the living room with her cupcake and her sunny yellow teacup and settled in.

Just three more weeks and Gail would be finished with radiation. Wayne had offered to take her to Las Vegas to celebrate after it was all over, but she simply wanted life to get back to normal. She wanted to help coordinate the fall book sale at the library, and she especially wanted to see that all the local shut-ins were equipped with a turkey and trimmings in time for Thanksgiving.

Gail turned on the TV in the living room just in time to see a commercial for the Promise of Pink, a benefit luncheon raising funds for breast cancer research. The luncheon was being held at the community center later in October. Maybe she would go this year.

Pink wasn't Gail's favorite color, but it represented what was fast becoming a new favorite cause. She raised her teacup in a silent toast to all those along the way who'd helped make it possible for her to have such a good prognosis. Then, she offered a prayer for all those facing a similar challenge and all those who would come behind her.

And then, just as any hope-filled woman would do, she ate her cupcake.

41
The Blossom

After washing the breakfast dishes, Miriam finished sipping her second cup of English Breakfast tea and headed outside to her garden with an anxious heart. After working so hard to create a magnificent display of fall annuals early last week, she had been dismayed when the Atlanta weather forecast had turned to rain, rain, and more rain. Added to all that rain, the area had suffered a sudden and violent storm the night before that was so powerful, it had caused trees to fall on houses and damage power lines.

Quite a few of her neighbors had flood damage in their basements, at least according to the e-mail circulated by her Sunday School class.

So while she knew she had much to be thankful for since she and Richard had suffered none of those calamities, she was still worried about her flowers and plants. Her *Camellia sinensis* bush had been struggling for weeks now, and she feared the storms might have finished it off for good. She hoped not.

Miriam slipped on her Crocs, the old blue gardening clogs she loved but that Richard had always said were "as ugly as homemade sin." She stepped outside and onto the back patio, trash bag in hand, fully prepared to find a hot mess awaiting her in the patio garden.

Instead, she was surprised to find that her annuals had fared pretty well. One of the new container gardens she'd planted had gotten knocked over in the storm, and the clay pot broke, but the plants themselves had landed right side up and still looked sturdy.

Miriam smiled as she realized that a broken pot didn't bother her nearly as much as a broken plant. In the raised flower beds near the patio, she had planted masses of mums in gold and yellow hues. She actually preferred the pink and mauve ones, yet she somehow believed that fall mums should echo the fall colors. This year, she'd also included a few bright orange marigolds in her garden plan. The marigolds wouldn't make it past the first freeze, but in the South, that could be a while.

Her one concession to a non-gold color was the purple asters. They were just as hardy as the mums, but Miriam knew they didn't like to be wet. She'd have to watch them to see whether they recovered from all the rain.

Miriam started to scoop up the broken pieces of the clay pot. She would break them into smaller pieces and recycle them, using them next spring to help with drainage in the bottom of new pots. She was halfway through cleaning up the broken pot when she glanced several yards away and saw something white bobbing in the wind near that *Camellia sinensis* bush she'd probably lost. Who knew what might have blown over into the yard in last night's storm.

Curious, Miriam stopped what she was doing and walked over to her beloved tea plant. To her astonishment, one perfect white blossom was there, so obviously, the plant wasn't dead after all.

Miriam stopped to finger the soft petals. The small white blossom reminded her of the Cherokee Rose, Georgia's state flower. Why on earth had her *Camellia sinensis* decided to blossom in such awful weather? But then Miriam remembered that she'd been out of town on a girlfriend getaway when the rain started, so the plant could have blossomed while she was still gone. And the last few times she'd been working in the garden, she was focused on the patio area and probably hadn't even looked at the tea plant. At any rate, that single blossom was quite lovely, she thought.

Back at the patio, Miriam finished cleaning up the spills from the storm and repotted the fallen plants. She kept an extra bag of potting soil on hand, and she always had a spare clay pot for container gardening too. She'd received so many passalong plants from friends over the years, Miriam knew it was wise to keep pots and soil on hand for those unexpected garden treasures that came her way.

Her *Camellia sinensis*, in fact, was a gift from a friend who bought it for her on a trip to North Carolina. A garden center there had the plants for sale, and Lynn had told Miriam that she had no idea whether the plant would thrive in Georgia, but since Miriam was such a tea lover, it seemed appropriate that she grow her own tea plant.

With a fine film of mist and dirt covering her hands and feet, Miriam went inside and took a quick shower. Her afternoon included, of all things, a planning meeting for her church's Christmas Tea. Christmas planning, already? Miriam sighed. She knew it wasn't too soon to start, although she would never be one of those women who had all her Christmas gifts purchased by July and wrapped by August.

Before she got busy with the rest of her day, Miriam decided to have a cup of Darjeeling, another of her favorite teas. She looked at the package and saw that it said, "Garden-fresh tea, straight from our tea gardens in Darjeeling."

Garden-fresh? No. Those tea leaves growing in her backyard, they were garden fresh. And to her great delight, despite the storm, they stood.

42
Just Say No

Sarah Harrison was feeling frazzled. Why was she always the one who got roped into doing the jobs no one else wanted? Just because she was a stay-at-home mom, everyone thought she had unlimited amounts of time, energy, and resources and could serve with the PTA, her sons' soccer leagues, and the church youth group.

Stay-at-home mom? By Sarah's calculations, the last time she'd actually stayed at home was one day in January when both boys were sick with the flu.

That morning, Sarah's day had started with an hour working the bake sale at Eli's school followed by another one-hour shift at the book fair at Logan's school. After ordering twenty-five dollars' worth of books Logan would probably never read so that he could win a "free" T-shirt, Sarah sped through McDonald's for a chicken biscuit. Her trusty travel mug with the "I Heart Tea" logo sat in her SUV's cup holder, and she was pleased that her ginger-flavored black tea was still fairly hot.

While stopped at a red light, Sarah whipped out her cellphone and typed *cereal* and *milk* on the list of grocery items she needed to pick up. The red light turned green, and the car behind her honked.

Sarah was tempted to let the driver know what she thought about that, but she was in a hurry, too, headed to the monthly committee meeting of the downtown merchants.

Brad Harrison, her husband, owned a small insurance agency downtown, and Sarah represented Harrison's Insurance Agency at the merchants' meetings. Sarah tried to switch gears from school fund-raising and think about her report to the merchants. She was in charge of coordinating refreshments for the downtown Christmas Open House. When she got to the meeting, the business owners were complaining about the parking situation and gossiping about the merchants who hadn't participated in the fall decorating contest.

I can't believe these people have nothing better to do than sit around worrying about whether their neighbor has a pumpkin outside the door. Sarah realized she'd been nervously bouncing her foot up and down when Mary Ellen Simpson, who owned a downtown florist, gave her a disapproving look. Mary Ellen lived for those monthly committee meetings and took seriously her position as president of the merchants' group.

Mary Ellen asked everyone to note a few dates of upcoming meetings, and some committee members pulled out their smartphones to add dates to their calendars. Sarah pretended to do the same, but actually she was typing *vitamins* onto her grocery list.

After Mary Ellen finally adjourned the interminably long meeting, she asked Sarah to stay behind. Mary Ellen wanted an update on the refreshments list for the Open House, which annoyed Sarah. If Mary Ellen didn't trust Sarah to do it, why assign her the job?

"You know, Sarah, I envy you," Mary Ellen said.

Sarah was surprised to hear that. "Really? Why would that be?"

"I'd love to just be a stay-at-home mom like you," she said. "It must be so nice to have all that time to yourself and do whatever you want all day. I tried that for a few years when my children were young, but I found myself going stir-crazy. Besides, I wanted to put my business degree to good use. But how nice for you that you can be a *homemaker.*"

"As a matter of fact—"

Sarah was about to give Mary Ellen a snippy response when Mary Ellen's phone rang. "Hi, Mayor Hudson," she said, pointing to her phone and mouthing "Excuse me" to Sarah.

Sarah rode home fuming. No one seemed to appreciate her volunteer work, and what was she really accomplishing?

That night after supper, Sarah told Brad about her day and repeated what Mary Ellen had said.

"If you don't enjoy volunteering, don't do it anymore," Brad said.

"Who will help coordinate the Christmas Open House next year if I don't?"

"They'll find someone else, or it won't get done. Either way, life will go on."

"Seriously?"

"Yes, I'm serious. You've been running around like crazy this past year, so why not take some time off and just say no to everything for a while? Might help you figure out what you really enjoy doing."

As Sarah prepared to load the dishwasher, her phone rang. She looked at the touchscreen. It was her friend Karen, the PTA president at Ethan's school.

Sarah picked up, and Karen said, "Hey, guess what? The nominating committee met, and they want you to be PTA president next year. Since there's never any opposition, I can meet with you sometime after Christmas to let you shadow me for the next few months and get ready to take over in May."

"Um, Karen, let me stop you right there. No," Sarah said.

"No?" Karen sounded confused. "What do you mean no?"

"I mean no, I'm not taking on any new projects right now."

"Are you sure?" Karen sounded genuinely puzzled.

"Yes, I'm sure."

Karen's voice lowered. "Is everything okay? Are you and Brad having problems?"

"Not at all," Sarah said. "But I'm burned out on volunteering and need to take a break. Maybe some other year, but not right now."

"Well, all right then," Karen said before hanging up.

Sarah felt slightly guilty, but it had felt great to tell someone no. Strangely, she didn't feel she owed anyone an explanation for her decision.

Next, she would try saying no to the soccer league.

As Sarah finished loading the top rack of the dishwasher, she popped in the travel tea mug she'd grown so used to sipping her tea from as she burned up the roads each day. Maybe she'd do like her mom and start drinking tea from a teacup instead.

Or maybe she'd have the neighbors over for tea. Maybe she'd start a tea business.

Then Sarah caught herself and smiled. *Or maybe I'll just read a book, or watch a TV program, or enjoy a cup of tea.*

She felt better already.

A Year of Teatime Tales

43
Teapot Ella

A long, long time ago, in a small town far, far away, there lived a beautiful teapot named Teapot Ella. Teapot Ella didn't know she was beautiful, however, because she was living with her teapot stepmother and her two teapot stepsisters in a dusty, nearly forgotten antique shop.

The stepmother, Teapot Hildegard, and the stepsisters, Teapot Myrt and Teapot Gert, were very unkind to Teapot Ella and constantly belittled her. In recent weeks, they'd seen her banished to the very back of the antique shop. She lived on the bottom shelf of the clearance rack. Sadly, few customers ever looked there.

Hildegard, Myrt, and Gert excelled at self-promotion and managed to worm their way into the antique shop's most prized spot, a lighted display case up front, where they preened and primped for passersby. They were quite proud of their steep price tags, even though it never occurred to the teapot ladies that those steep prices were keeping them prisoners in the shop. Their lofty estimations of their own worth, however, were all it took to keep them happy.

Then one day, there appeared two women who had never visited that antique shop before, Grace and Mercy. The two had been out visiting a friend when they decided to take a peek into the dusty little shop.

"Oh, look, girls," said Hildegard, straightening up. "These two women are new here, and maybe one of them will want to take us all home with them! Myrt, Gert, turn around. Smile. Yes, show them your stuff, girls."

Myrt elbowed Gert with her handle, and Gert got her back with a swift tap to the spout.

"I saw that," said Hildegard. "Behave, girls. Do you want to get sent to the clearance shelf with Teapot Ella?"

The girls laughed uproariously. No antique shop owner in her right mind would send teapots as beautiful as they were back with the lowly specimens like Teapot Ella.

As usual, the teapots in the front case got the visitors' attention almost immediately.

"Grace, look at this amazing red and gold teapot," said Mercy. "Those stripes are so bold and vivid, and that gold trim is absolutely perfect. And look, these purple and green ones nearby are just as ornate!"

"I see what you mean," said Grace, "but they're just a little *too* perfect." Then she whispered in a low voice so the shop owner couldn't hear, "They're a little on the gaudy side for me. Kind of stuffy."

Hildegard sniffed in disdain when she heard that comment. Amateurs. Clearly, those women didn't know a quality teapot when they saw one. Their loss.

Grace and Mercy slowly meandered through the shop, stopping to sort through vintage linens and recipe booklets. Mercy found a pretty blue apron she liked, and Grace found a couple of old cookie recipe booklets to inspire her Christmas baking. They were almost finished browsing when Mercy said, "Look, a clearance rack."

Grace stepped over to see what her friend had found and immediately scanned the shelves. She stooped down and pulled out something she'd spotted on the bottom shelf. "Mercy, check this out!"

Grace held up a beautiful pink teapot that was missing its lid. The softly colored rose design was quite becoming, and Grace blew on the teapot, dislodging a small film of dust.

"No lid?" said Mercy.

Grace shook her head. "I guess that's why it's on clearance." But Grace kept looking and spotted what certainly looked like a lid stuck back in a corner of that same shelf. She gently placed it on the teapot, and it was a perfect match. It was the loveliest teapot Grace had ever seen.

She held it up, and Mercy said, "You found the lid? It's meant to be, then."

Soon, the women were standing at the checkout counter in the middle of the store and paying for their purchases. The shop owner was handing over Mercy's change when all three women heard a squeal and a creak from the front of the store. Three heads turned.

Then, a shattering sound filled the air. All eyes turned to that lighted display case. The glass shelf displaying the three teapots Mercy and Grace had seen earlier had suddenly crashed onto the shelf below. The women rushed up in time to see a sad, broken mixture of red, purple, and green porcelain.

Teapot Ella, already wrapped and inside a plastic bag, couldn't see what had happened, but she feared the worst. For months now, she'd heard the shop owner telling her husband the hinge on that shelf was about to give way. Teapot Ella had warned her stepmother and stepsisters, but they had laughed off her concerns. Teapot Ella hoped she hadn't just heard the muffled cries of their demise.

As Grace was saying her goodbyes to Mercy that afternoon, she added, "You know, I've always wanted a special vintage teapot that was prettier than any other, and I can't believe I just found her back there for a song."

As she was carefully ushered into her new home, Teapot Ella was excited to think of the new life she was about to begin. She wondered if there would be other teawares and whether they would accept her into the family.

With a soft thud, Teapot Ella was placed on the kitchen counter and released from the layers of tissue that had surrounded her. To her delight, she looked up into the face of the most tall, dark, and handsome electric teakettle she had ever seen.

"Prince Warming!" she cried.

Teapot Ella's new owner rinsed her out with warm water, added a few teaspoons of loose leaf tea, and pressed a button on Prince Warming. Soon, he and Teapot Ella were making beautiful tea together. All the unhappiness of her past was forgotten in the joy of being paired with the teakettle she'd waited her whole life to meet.

And they lived happily ever after.

A Year of Teatime Tales

⁓ 44 ⁓
Time Change

The wind howled, knocking a tree branch against the window behind the living room sofa where Debbie sat, and she jumped. A little after eight o'clock and she'd seen only a handful of trick-or-treaters, mostly children from the neighborhood.

Scott was in Chicago for a tech conference that weekend, and their twin daughters were both at their respective colleges until Thanksgiving, so Debbie was home alone that Halloween night.

A low rumble sounded, and Debbie hoped a storm wasn't about to hit. She hated storms, and she especially hated storms in the fall and winter, when the nights were already so long and dark.

A sudden streak of lightning shone into the room, and an earth-shaking clap of thunder came a few seconds later, causing Debbie to finally close the new novel she'd been trying to read. Maybe a nice cup of tea would calm her nerves.

She turned on the light in the kitchen and immediately screamed. A small spider was hanging from the ceiling by a thread, mere inches from her face. She batted away the strand, but when she looked for the spider, it had disappeared, which made her uneasy. She knew the spider was probably harmless, but she detested insects of any kind. Where there was one, there might be another.

Debbie wished Scott was there to kill it for her. Although she hated spiders, she also hated the thought of one crawling up on her, so she refused to even get near them herself. Maybe that spider went up under the dishwasher. With any luck, it would curl up and die.

After she caught her breath, she filled her electric teakettle and waited a few minutes for the water to boil. She knew she would be up a while thanks to the storm whirling around the house, so she went ahead and made a whole pot of Pumpkin Spice Tea. She was using the vintage teapot she'd found at an antique mall over the summer, a brown teapot shaped like a clock. It read "Tea for Two," its hands permanently fixed in the two o'clock position.

Debbie wondered if there was something significant about the two o'clock time on that teapot clock face since, traditionally, teatime was at four p.m. Probably, it was simply a nod to the "two" in the phrase "tea for two."

That year, Halloween also happened to fall on the night that Daylight Saving Time ended for the year. As an English teacher, Debbie was somewhat obsessed about calling it, correctly, Daylight Saving Time instead of the more commonly used Daylight Savings Time. "When it goes into effect each spring, you're not *savings* time, you're *saving* time," she always told her students. Of course, most high school students didn't care at all about the time change, much less the grammar surrounding it.

After her tea steeped for four minutes, Debbie returned to the living room. By then it was after nine, so she felt safe in turning off the porch lights. Few trick-or-treaters ever came after nightfall, but none would come in a thunderstorm.

The lightning came faster, and the thunder came louder, but Debbie sipped her Pumpkin Spice Tea and tried to focus on her novel. Then, a bolt of lightning penetrated the living room sheers, bathing the room in an electric white glow. And then ... darkness.

"That's just great," Debbie said to the empty room. "Guess it's time for some candles."

She easily made her way to the kitchen, and as she reached into the drawer where she kept matches and flashlights, she remembered the spider she'd seen earlier. A chill ran down her spine, but she had no choice except to reach quickly into the drawer for the flashlight. Thank goodness it worked.

Holding the flashlight in one hand, Debbie used the other to root around in the drawer for that long-handled lighter she used to light candles. When she lighted her new cinnamon-and-apple-scented candle, she would at least have light to read by.

The thunder and lightning continued, but the intensity was waning. With the warm glow of candlelight near her seat in the living room, she managed to pull herself back into her novel. She cuddled up beneath a soft throw in a corner of the couch and decided to close her eyes for just a few minutes.

The next thing Debbie knew, she was startled awake by the sound of an electrical hum and the reappearance of light from the lamps in the room. She rubbed her eyes. The clock on the mantel read three o'clock, but since she hadn't changed it yet, that meant it was really just two o'clock thanks to the time change.

She massaged the crick in her neck. Clearly, she needed to head down the hall and get to bed.

First, though, she carried her empty teacup into the kitchen and rinsed out the brown clock face teapot.

Only ... the teapot's hands were pointing to three o'clock, not two o'clock.

What?

Debbie stared at the teapot.

I know that teapot read two o'clock earlier, she thought. She shook her head. Her mind was playing tricks on her, clearly.

Shaking off the strange feeling about the teapot, Debbie headed to her bedroom and dressed for bed. She would pick up Scott from the airport in just a few more hours, and she couldn't wait. She always felt safer when he was around.

Meanwhile, back in the kitchen, a small black spider crawled out from his home beneath the dishwasher and slowly made his way up the counter and onto the vintage brown teapot.

He climbed onto the clock face, which was still a little slippery thanks to that soapy rinse, and heaved and panted as he pushed the hands back into the two o'clock position.

"Time change," he said.

And with that, the spider skirted back to his hideaway beneath the dishwasher, where he would remain until spring.

~ 45 ~
High Tea

Lynn, Nan, Bernie, Felice, and Mary were beside themselves. A full-page ad in the *Colorado Springs Daily News* touted a local charity's "high tea" planned for that Christmas. The five longtime friends, out enjoying their monthly custom of gathering at a local tearoom, bemoaned the fact that the good people of their area persisted in referring to afternoon tea as high tea.

Lynn, a recently retired tearoom owner, pantomimed banging her head on a table. "I've flat given up," she said. "I called mine afternoon tea for years, even explained what high tea is, and yet women called me every single week wanting to make reservations for high tea. Every. Single. Week."

Nan, a certified tea educator who taught classes on teatime, said she would continue to teach that afternoon tea was the leisurely afternoon tea meal consisting of savories, sweets, and scones. "And yes, I will continue to tell them that high tea is actually a lowbrow affair that was taken at a high dining table, a meal consisting not of tea sandwiches and scones but of meats, cheese, and the like."

"You're not educating them fast enough," said Bernie, short for Bernadette, a registered nurse. "Every time I wear my teapot pin on my scrubs at the hospital, I get asked if I've ever been to high tea. I once tried to correct a patient, but when some middle-aged woman is trying to recover from a heart attack, it's not a good idea to get her riled up over the definition of high tea."

"Humph," said Felice, an accountant. "They're going to give *me* a heart attack if they don't quit calling it high tea!"

Mary, a retired teacher, just smiled and didn't say a word.

"Why are you so quiet, Mary?" said Bernie. "Usually, you're madder than anyone when people refer to afternoon tea as high tea."

"Ladies, I have a plan," Mary said.

"I'm all ears," said Felice. "Spill it."

Mary looked around, and all eyes were on her. "Now our state's been in the news ever since marijuana was legalized for recreational use a few years back, right?"

"Yes, but what's that got to do with anything?" Lynn said.

"How many middle-aged women like us are into marijuana?"

"Well, now, there was that one time that I—"

"Don't go there, Felice," said Mary. "We don't need to be reminded of how you 'experimented' back in college. That doesn't count. We're talking about regular marijuana use here."

The others looked on, intrigued, and Mary continued. "Just think about it. What if we convinced everyone that high tea really meant ... HIGH tea!"

"How would we do that?" Bernie asked.

"Easy," Mary said. "We're going to use our powers for good and spread a rumor that high tea is really just code for a good old-fashioned pot party. And what proper afternoon-tea-loving gal is going to go for that?"

"I don't know," said Nan. "We know that's not really what high tea is ..."

"Yeah, and look how far that's gotten us," said Lynn. "I'm in."

"Me too," said Felice. "If it gets everyone to stop calling afternoon tea high tea, then I'm all for it."

Slowly, the others came around.

"We'll start with the tearoom owners," said Mary.

"But the tearoom owners already know what high tea is, they just don't know how to politely inform their customers," said Lynn. "Believe me, I know. I've talked to plenty of them about it over the years. They're so afraid of offending someone, it's easier for them to remain silent."

"I think most women want to know what's correct," said Nan. "I don't think those tearoom owners are giving them enough credit."

Soon, a plan unfolded. Mary assigned each of the women a tearoom or two to call and inquire whether it was true that they offered high tea. If the tearoom owner said yes, then the woman asked her to describe the menu. If the "high tea" menu included typical afternoon tea fare, the caller would say, "Oh, I always thought that was called afternoon tea. My women's club heard that high tea referred to teas where they serve marijuana brownies and things like that. You're sure your tearoom is on the up-and-up?"

Naturally, some of the tearoom owners were horrified that patrons might think they were engaging in anything even remotely scandalous.

The next month, the five friends met again at a local tearoom and filled each other in on their campaign to curb the misuse of the term "high tea."

Felice said one tearoom owner had hung up on her, thinking the call was a prank, but Lynn and Bernie both had good responses from businesswomen who suddenly wanted to clarify that what they offered was actually afternoon tea, not high tea.

Mary had called the newspaper that ran the "High Tea" ad and asked for the advertising director, then inquired if he knew whether high tea was referring to marijuana use at that upcoming charity tea. There in the tearoom, she whipped out for her friends a full-page ad for the festive Christmas event suddenly featuring "English Afternoon Tea" rather than the "High Tea" advertised earlier.

"We're obviously starting to make some headway here, so I think we need to do something to celebrate," said Mary. She turned to her friends, who were all sipping tea from their bone china teacups. "Suggestions?"

"Yes," said Bernie. "I think we should have a true high tea!"

"Perfect," agreed Nan. "Let's decide on a menu while we're all here."

And soon enough, the ladies were offering to prepare meat pies, hot buttered toast, plain scones, fruit, cheese, chocolate cake, and other foods for the meal.

"To high tea," said Mary, holding her teacup aloft.

Four others quickly joined her, lightly clinking their cups together and laughing as they said, "To high tea!"

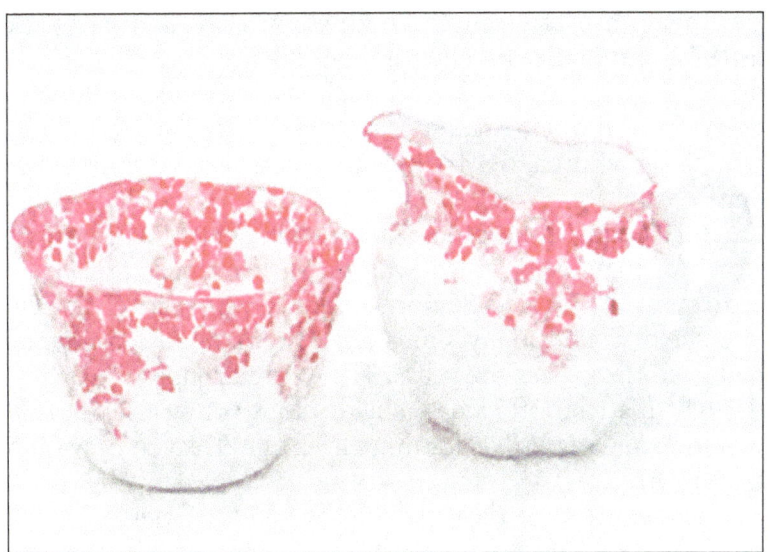

46
Knickknacks

Louise had hoped such a day would never come, but after she had taken one fall too many, her children had insisted it was time for her to either move in with one of them—a fate she saw as worse than death—or move to that upscale new "independent living facility" in town. They could call it whatever they liked, but "old folks' home" was what it was.

How did I get to be eighty-seven so quickly? I don't feel eighty-seven on the inside. And I'm a very young and healthy eighty-seven, nothing like all those old people who live at Sunrise Senior Living. Louise shook her head. It seemed like only yesterday that she was growing up on a farm out in the country, then going to primary school, junior high, and high school. After secretarial school, she met the man she would marry, the love of her life, Ronald Fairchild. Together, they'd had a wonderful life. Ronald was president of the local bank, and when their two daughters and a son came along, Louise stayed home to raise the children.

Ronald had tragically been killed by a drunk driver back in 1977, and Louise had thought her life was over. To her surprise, the grief subsided—although she still missed Ronald, every day—and she created a new life for herself, one built around her church, her friends, her clubs, and of course, her family.

But today, she would start packing away a lifetime's worth of memories and downsize to that small, pricy new apartment at Sunrise Senior Living. It was a lovely place, one she'd visited many times since so many of her friends had lived there over the years. They were dropping like flies, though. Just the other day, she'd told a young friend, who was in her sixties, "I've got more friends in Heaven now than I do down here."

How many more days did she have on earth herself? Only Heaven knew. She was in good health, her bursitis notwithstanding, and unlike some of her friends who liked to moan about their aches and pains, Louise simply pretended hers didn't exist. It didn't make them any less real, but it helped her not to focus on them. Besides, who wanted to hear about someone else's aches and pains anyway?

She massaged her shoulder and went back to sorting through some of the paperwork she'd accumulated over the years. As she flipped past another yellowed newspaper clipping, she paused to study a new age spot on her wrinkled hands. Too bad the cosmetics companies could never come up with a good solution for age spots. Or wrinkles, for that matter.

She had kept her Christmas card lists for the past fifty years, and she enjoyed reading over the names. Then she smiled as she came across an invitation to the 1964 Women's Civic League Ball. She could still remember Ronald in his handsome new tuxedo and how it complemented her black-and-white-striped gown from Lord and Taylor. Those were happy times indeed.

Then, Louise came across a stapled stack of papers titled simply "Bridge Club." She got a faraway look in her eyes. After Ron Jr., Carol, and Lillian were in school, Louise got more involved in the community. She sat on boards and volunteered for various causes, and then she was invited to join her mother-in-law's bridge club. Louise hadn't known whether to be thrilled or offended. The most well-connected women in town were in that bridge club, but they were also the oldest women in town. Most of them, including her mother-in-law, had long since passed.

Louise shrugged. She refused to spend too much time mourning those who'd "crossed over," as she liked to say. Instead, her mind's eye went to the little Craftsman-style cottage at 17 Burton St. where her mother-in-law had hosted countless bridge parties.

She rose from her living room chair and walked over to her china cabinet. She looked in the back right corner on the second shelf. Yes, there it was, that Dainty Pink sugar bowl and creamer by Shelley.

That was the set her mother-in-law had used at bridge club for nearly thirty years, and when she got to where she couldn't play bridge anymore, she had passed it on to Louise. The Shelley set was so lovely. Louise reached in and removed the cream pitcher. Eggshell thin but surprisingly strong, it had served beautifully at all of Mother Fairchild's bridge parties and then, later, those hosted by Louise herself.

"Mother, why don't you get rid of those old knickknacks?" Lillian had asked one day.

"Yes, Mom. Sunrise has nice dinnerware for you to use if you decide to host a party. You won't need those knickknacks there," Carol had agreed.

"Knickknacks," they called them.

I may be eighty-seven, but I'm not dead yet, and I fully intend to live with the things I love until my last dying breath, Louise thought.

She knew they were only "things," but that Dainty Pink sugar and creamer were her last visible ties to some of the people she'd loved most. Get rid of her knickknacks? Not hardly.

A knock sounded at the door, and Louise went to open it. "Hi there, sweetheart," she said, giving Ron Jr. a kiss on the cheek. Ron, a banker like his dad, had told her he'd come over on his lunch hour to take her to sign the papers that would make her the newest resident of Sunrise Senior Living.

"Are you ready, Mom?"

"Ready as I'll ever be," she said.

In one more week, she would have to pack up all those memories and oversee their transport to the new place. It would be tiring, but she knew she could do it. And like that Dainty Pink sugar and creamer, she was much stronger than she looked.

47
A Family Thanksgiving

Was it wrong to be glad your sister-in-law couldn't come to Thanksgiving dinner? Kathy felt guilty, but secretly, she was thrilled that Lisa, wife of her older brother, Ted, would be away on her girlfriends' cruise and couldn't make it.

Lisa was so competitive. No matter what was being discussed, Lisa could top it. If Kathy was praised for a recipe, Lisa knew how to make one that was tastier. If one of Kathy's children had earned an honor in high school, Lisa's college-age children had earned something better. No matter how hard Kathy worked to make Thanksgiving special, Lisa always managed to spoil the day.

That year, no Lisa at Thanksgiving meant no drama, and Kathy was so pleased. Even after waking at five a.m. on

Thanksgiving so she could stick her hand up a half-frozen turkey's rear end to get it ready for baking, she was humming Christmas tunes and cheerfully assembling sweet potato casseroles when Stan got up.

"Why are you in such a good mood?" he asked.

"No reason," Kathy said.

The doorbell rang at eleven a.m., and Kathy was still humming when she opened the door to find Ted on her doorstep—until she saw Lisa beside him.

"Darling," said Lisa, air-kissing Kathy. "Our ship had engine trouble, so all of us on the girlfriends' cruise made it home for Thanksgiving. I told Ted it would be a surprise."

"It certainly is," Kathy said.

"Besides, I didn't want you to worry about having enough food. I don't eat as much as you all anyway, you know." Lisa was fond of letting the family know that her "fat" clothes were a size four.

Kathy laughed. "It's Thanksgiving, Lisa. One more mouth would hardly be noticed around here."

"Oh, you're sweet," she said, "but I do remember that year you ran out of dessert, and Ted couldn't have that second piece of pumpkin pie he wanted. Ah, family memories. Right?"

"Right," Kathy said, grimacing. "If you'll excuse me, I need to check on the turkey."

"No problem. I know how hard you try to cook one that's not too dry," Lisa said.

Kathy bit her lip and walked away. She had a troubled look on her face as she scooted Stan away from his nibbling around the stove.

"Something wrong?" he said.

"Just something Lisa said," she replied.

"Honey, don't let her get to you. If you can't ignore her, just give it right back to her. There's no use letting her ruin your Thanksgiving."

Suddenly, Kathy thought, *He's right*.

By noon, the dining room was full, and everyone was standing around enjoying appetizers. In addition to Stan and Kathy and their teenage sons, Sean, fifteen, and Lee, thirteen, there were Ted, Lisa, Stan's parents, Kathy and Ted's parents, and three assorted aunts. Stan's Aunt Mabel, a real sweetheart, had already complimented Kathy on setting the dessert table with the pretty harvest-themed teapot Mabel had given her as a hostess gift last Thanksgiving. Kathy had known Mabel would notice that. Every time Kathy used the teapot, she recalled the gracious woman who had given it to her. Soon, everyone was seated around the table. Stan blessed the meal and carved the turkey, which Kathy noted was slicing with ease.

"Mmm," said Ted. "This is the best turkey you've ever made, sis."

"Yeah," said Sean. "Dad, can you cut me another slice?"

"Can I have another roll?" asked Lee.

"Kathy, your green been casserole is especially tasty this year," said Aunt Mabel. "Did you grow the green beans?"

"Oh, heavens no. Those are straight from the produce aisle of Kroger," Kathy said.

"If you want some good green beans, the organic ones at Publix are great," Lisa said. "They're not that much more than the ones on sale at Kroger."

Kathy had had enough. She cleared her throat, took a sip of her iced tea, and said, "Lisa, what's really bothering you?"

Lisa sounded surprised. "Bothering me? Nothing's bothering me. Why would you say that?"

The men around the table looked nervous. The women looked intrigued.

"Every year, you make these comments about the meal, or the house, or the groceries, and I'm just wondering if I've done something to upset you." Kathy's voice wasn't shaking, her face wasn't red, and she was perfectly in control. It felt great. "If I've done something to bother you, let's clear the air and get it settled. If I haven't, then what can I do to get you to stop your criticism?"

"I have no idea what you're talking about," Lisa said, getting up from the table with a stunned look on her face. "I'm feeling rather nauseated, probably because I've just returned from sea. I'm sorry, but I don't think I'll be able to finish this meal. I think we need to go, Ted."

Looking embarrassed, Ted rose from the table.

"Are you sure that's all it is?" Kathy asked.

"I'm sure," Lisa said. "Please forgive me."

Kathy looked her in the eye and said, "Of course I forgive you." And to her brother, she said, "Let me at least send you home with some food. We've got enough to feed an army."

She sent Ted and Lisa off with a shopping bag full of Tupperware and then returned to the table. Everyone seemed to be having a wonderful time.

After lunch, the men headed off to watch ballgames while the women helped tidy up. Mabel walked over and squeezed her arm. "You handled that beautifully, dear."

Kathy smiled. "Did I?"

"Lisa has never had anyone stand up to her, and you did it kindly but firmly. It was just what she needed."

"Thank you," Kathy said. "That means a lot coming from you, Aunt Mabel."

Mabel gave her another squeeze and said brightly, "Now, let's use that pretty teapot to make us all a nice pot of cranberry tea—to celebrate a *most* happy Thanksgiving."

"I'll drink to that," Kathy said. And she did.

A Year of Teatime Tales

～ 48 ～
Lunching at the Swan Coach House

The week after Thanksgiving, Monica and Julie met for lunch at the Swan Coach House in Atlanta, just as they had for years. An elegant restaurant, gift shop, and art gallery, the Swan Coach House boasted an old-fashioned tearoom ambience and was one of their favorite places to catch up with each other before the busyness of the holidays. In a former life, the space had served as the carriage house for the Inman family estate, Atlanta's iconic Swan House, but today, the coach house was a beautifully appointed restaurant where the Atlanta blue hairs—and women from all over the region, as well as the well-informed tourists—enjoyed having lunch.

The middle-aged woman serving them took their beverage orders—hot tea for Monica, ice water with lemon for Julie—and delivered a small basket of bite-size breads for them to nibble while deciding on lunch.

"Did you see their new silver trays in the gift shop?" said Julie. "I love the one that says 'Merry Christmas, Y'all.'"

"You must have gotten here early," Monica said. "With the traffic this morning, I barely made it in time to meet you, so I haven't more than glanced at the gift shop yet."

"You better have your credit card handy, because you will go *crazy* in that gift shop," Julie said. She took a sip of her ice water and paused to look at her friend. "I know how you are about Christmas decorations. You still can't resist them, can you?"

"This year, actually, I can," Monica said, adding a packet of sugar to her tea.

Julie looked puzzled. "This year? What do you mean, this year? Are you and Alan going out of town for Christmas?"

"No," Monica said.

"Then why are you going to be able to resist the Christmas decorations?"

"Because I'm not buying any more new decorations for Christmas."

"Since when?"

The server returned for their orders, so the conversation paused. "I'll have the Swan's Favorite," Monica said. The restaurant's signature dish was chicken salad served in timbales—deliciously light pastry shells—along with a slice of their creamy, jewel-toned frozen fruit salad and Swan Coach House cheese straws. Julie ordered the spinach quiche, which also came with cheese straws.

As soon as the server left, Julie pressed, "Spill it. What's up with this no-new-decorations thing? You like to decorate for Christmas more than any woman I know."

"I've got a bet going with Alan. He bet me a weekend in Chicago that I couldn't go the whole Christmas season without buying any new decorations."

"Is it worth it?" Julie swirled the water and ice around in her glass and took a sip.

"Sure it is. It's not as if I need anything new. Besides, the season will technically be over December 31, and if there's anything I really want, I can probably find it on clearance somewhere. It's win-win for me, because I'll save enough for a real splurge when we get to Chicago."

"I don't know. What if you see some Christmas decoration you just love? It sounds risky," Julie said.

And then their orders arrived on the restaurant's pretty green china. Monica commented on how the presentation was always absolutely perfect whenever they ate at the Swan Coach House. She said her colorful plate of food had a simple southern elegance she absolutely adored, and Julie quickly agreed.

"So, I guess you'll be staying out of stores this Christmas?" Julie said.

"Not at all," Monica replied.

"Isn't that going to be torture for you?"

"Not really. It's just going to be a lesson in delayed gratification. That, plus I've always found a way to bend the rules a little." Monica grinned as she took another bite of her chicken salad. "Mmm. I hope they don't ever stop making this."

Julie was already halfway through her spinach quiche. "I know what you mean," she said. "Say"—she tapped the plastic display stand on their table—"are you going to one of their Christmas teas here this year?"

"I haven't really thought about it," Monica said. "Why? Do you want to go?"

"Yes. Let's make reservations for that last one right before Christmas. Besides, you'll need some therapy after going almost a whole Christmas season without buying any new decorations."

When the women were nearly finished with their meals, the server stopped by to see if they wanted dessert. As was their custom, both ordered the famous French Silk Swan. A meringue base was topped with a filling of chocolate cream cheese mouse, all surrounded by whipped cream and then embellished with slivered almonds and swan heads made of pastry dough. The desserts had about a zillion calories each, but they were worth it.

After paying their bill and leaving a tip for the server, the women headed out. Julie paused at the entrance to the gift shop. "I don't suppose you want to shop today, do you?"

"Why not?" said Monica. "You said they had some nice new silver trays." Monica walked past Julie to a table topped with glistening silver gifts. "Oh, this is darling!" she said, picking up the scalloped-edge tray with "Merry Christmas, Y'all" engraved in the center. "I think I'll get one of these for Alan's mother. She'll love it. And of course I want one for me too."

Julie shook her head. "So you're giving up on that weekend in Chicago?"

"Not at all," said Monica. "Look." She grabbed a linen tea towel, draped it across the center of the tray, and plucked a glittering ornament of faux grapes from a neighboring display. "There. It's not a Christmas decoration. It's simply a pretty silver tray for home decor, perfect for year-round entertaining."

"Isn't that cheating on your bet?" Julie said.

"Hey, what happens in the gift shop, stays in the gift shop," Monica said.

And so, fueled by cheese straws and laughter, the women browsed the beloved local shop, just as they always had—and always would.

49
"Ho, ho, ho! Merry Christmas!"

Gilda Donnelly rapped her gavel on the podium to open the Fortieth Annual Convention of the International Santa Claus Mug Collectors Society. "Ladies and gentlemen, if I may have your attention, please."

The lights in the ballroom blinked off and on twice, signaling it was time for the opening of the group's highly anticipated fortieth anniversary convention.

"Ladies and gentlemen, on behalf of the International Santa Claus Mug Collectors Society, it is my privilege to welcome you to the beautiful city of Orlando!"

The audience responded with hearty applause, and Gilda smiled and joined in. She was thrilled for the chance to leave chilly Chicago behind for the weekend and enjoy a trip to sunny central Florida.

Once she had everyone's attention, Gilda explained Friday afternoon's schedule. For the first time, organizers had decided not to distribute convention programs until after the welcome session. Otherwise, they knew, many attendees would skip the welcome and go straight to the afternoon sessions. This year's offerings included The History of Santa Claus Mugs, How to Value a Santa Claus Mug Collection for Insurance Purposes, Crafting a Creative Santa Claus Mug Display, and the session she would lead, Santa Claus Mugs and Their Role in Popular Culture.

Also new this year was an afternoon Hot Chocolate Social at which the attendees would receive their Official Commemorative Santa Claus Mug. An artist in Scotland had won the competition to design this year's mug, and Santa's famous red hat featured a band of Scottish tartan.

No other Santa Claus mugs in the world, however, meant as much to Gilda as the three she'd kept from childhood. Her family—her father and mother, her three older brothers, and Gilda—had always posed for a Christmas Eve photo in their new Christmas pajamas, Santa mugs in hand. Most of those beloved mugs had been broken or tossed out over the years, so Gilda treasured the one she had convinced her mother to give her. In addition to that one, she had two child-sized Santa mugs she had used with her dolls.

Gilda's mugs were some of the ones on display in the exhibit hall. Each year, convention goers were invited to showcase their favorite Santa mugs, and anyone who wanted to could include a brief story about their mugs in the event program.

Since Gilda had been serving as president of the collectors' society for three years, all but the newest attendees were familiar with her three treasured mugs. Still, each year, someone came up to her to say how much they appreciated the fact that she had kept the mementos of childhood. Many of the attendees wished they had their own childhood Santa mugs. Often, it was that nostalgia that caused someone to begin collecting the mugs in the first place.

Like Marilee Hopkins of Australia, who still had her first

childhood Santa mug. Marilee had more than three thousand Santa Claus mugs at last count, with no duplicates allowed. She loved to find the primitive-looking ones that some unknown woman had created in ceramics class. She devoted hours to visiting online auction sites to make sure she didn't miss one.

The afternoon's four sessions were held simultaneously, and each session would be repeated three more times before the end of the convention the next day. That way, attendees had the opportunity to participate in all four sessions if they wanted.

During the afternoon's Hot Chocolate Social, Gilda walked over to the beverage station and looked for the basket of teas. Not everyone liked hot chocolate, so coffee and tea were always offered as well. The convention committee knew Gilda was partial to peppermint tea.

The afternoon of programs went off without a hitch. That evening, everyone gathered for a banquet where they enjoyed a concert of Christmas carols, ate a traditional Christmas meal, and honored the officers and volunteers who had served the organization over the past year.

At the end of the long day, Gilda headed back to her room and sipped a cup of tea from one of her newer Santa mugs. One year, a reporter interviewing her about the convention noticed she was sipping her tea from a paper cup, and his article took delight in noting that the president of a Santa Claus mug collectors group didn't always use her Santa Claus mugs. Never again, she had vowed. Not when she had about three hundred Santa Claus mugs of her own.

The next morning, Gilda and the others headed back to the meeting rooms to repeat the programming from the day before. As always, it was a fun but frenzied time of leading the sessions, seeing old friends, making new ones, and answering hundreds of questions about Santa Claus mugs.

Finally, everyone gathered back in the ballroom for Saturday's closing session. One of the highlights of the convention each year came when a charitable gift was made in the name of one lucky attendee. All the names were printed on slips of paper and placed in a large papier mâché Santa Claus mug. Gilda reached in and stirred the entries. To be sure the newcomers understood how the drawing worked, she explained what she was doing. "Each year, in the spirit of giving, we like to conclude by choosing one attendee who receives a five-hundred-dollar donation to the charity of their choice. And this year's winner is"—she paused for dramatic emphasis—"Richard Merriman of Nashville, Tennessee!"

Everyone clapped as Richard headed to the stage. "But first," Gilda said, "he has to prove he knows the magic words." She spoke into the microphone and asked, "Richard, what are they?"

Slowly, he replied, "Ho. Ho. Ho. Merry. Christmas!"

"That's correct, Richard, and according to what you wrote on your registration form, the donation this year goes to the Salvation Army. Congratulations!"

Gilda pounded her gavel again. "And now, it is my pleasure to lead everyone in closing our meeting with those same magic words. And they are?"

"Ho, ho, ho! Merry Christmas!"

50
The Baptists and Christmas Tea

The Tea Society had just left my house after our annual Christmas Tea, and my dear friend Mary Lou Carter had stayed behind to help with cleanup. But first, I prepared us a nice big pot of Twinings Christmas Tea.

"I love the little tags on these tea bags," said Mary Lou. "But I thought you only drank loose leaf tea. What gives?"

"Lots of ladies in the Tea Society give me Christmas tea bags each year, and I'm happy to have them. In fact, I'm saving some of them for when I help Starla Mooneyham at our Women's Ministry Christmas Tea next Saturday."

Mary Lou suddenly snorted some tea. She made a mess when she tried to clean it up, thoroughly staining one of my nice red napkins I had so carefully folded to look like Christmas roses. Not that I minded. I always said it was my pleasure to have friends enjoy my nice things.

"*You*, Brenda Johnson, are helping *the* Starla Mooneyham, head of the Women's Ministry, with the Christmas Tea?" Mary Lou sputtered. "Last I checked, you had forsaken the Baptist church and were becoming an Episcopalian after speaking at their big fall tea."

I always tried to keep my opinions to myself, but I was about to tell Mary Lou that she really needed to keep up if she wanted to know what was going on in town. "Now I *know* I told you what happened at that tea."

"The food was bad?"

"No, it wasn't bad at all," I said. "They had some wonderful tea sandwiches, including my Waldorf Chicken Salad on Mini Croissants—the ones they featured in *Southern Lady* magazine—and a cute little sandwich with fancy cucumber slices on top. Their scones were even served with real clotted cream someone had brought back from England."

"Then refresh my memory. What was the problem?" Mary Lou said.

"They advertised my program topic as … high tea," I said.

Mary Lou just shook her head and reached for some of the chocolate truffles left over from the afternoon's tea.

"So how did you hook up with Starla Mooneyham?"

"It was the oddest thing," I said. "You probably don't remember this, but earlier this year, Starla had turned up her nose at my chicken salad sandwiches—"

"Oh, I do remember," interrupted Mary Lou. "That's why you got mad and left the church to begin with."

"I did *not* get mad," I said, but Mary Lou was making me mad by not letting me finish. "Anyway, right after the Episcopal ladies' tea, Starla called me one day in a panic. She said the secretary of the Women's Ministry had accidentally ordered two thousand oversized plastic plates for the Christmas Tea. Starla said all the finger sandwiches looked puny on such a large plate, so she thought my Waldorf Chicken Salad on Mini Croissants would look pretty and take up more room."

Mary Lou polished off another truffle and wiped chocolate off her fingers with my pretty red napkin. I reminded myself that it was my joy to share my nice things with others.

"Hey, is that a new teacup?" she said. She pointed at my English teacup with holly berries on it. I told her it was an early Christmas gift from Starla, who was thanking me for helping rescue the Christmas Tea.

Mary Lou just nodded.

Something about Mary Lou's attitude had shifted, but I couldn't put my finger on it. She said she was glad I was "returning to the fold," but she didn't seem as happy as I expected that I was going back to being a Baptist.

Mary Lou helped me wash and put away all the china, and she gathered up the napkins that had been folded into roses earlier in the day, including the one she had smeared the chocolate all over, not that I really minded.

I told Mary Lou I wanted her to sit at the table with Starla and me at the Christmas Tea next Saturday. She said she would, but she didn't seem too excited about it.

"So now you and Starla are tight?" she said.

"Not really. Why?"

"First you're helping her with the tea, then she's bringing you a nice teacup for Christmas. I just wondered if she was going to be your new BFF of teatime, that's all."

That was when I realized it: Mary Lou was jealous. So I reached over and covered her hand with my own. "Starla Mooneyham's a nice enough person, and I'm happy she finally came to her senses about using my recipe for the church tea, but she could never replace you as my best tea friend. Why, do you know, Starla asked me if I collected tea *diffusers* last week when the tea committee met."

"Diffusers!" Mary Lou chortled. "She means *infusers!*"

"Yes," I said. "And she originally wanted to advertise the Christmas Tea as 'high tea' until I explained things to her."

"For Heaven's sake," Mary Lou said, perking up.

Soon, we finished tidying up after the day's tea. Mary Lou was headed out the door when she turned and said, "Will you and Cliff be home tomorrow evening before church? I'll be out delivering my holiday jars of pimiento cheese spread, and I'd like to bring yours by if that's okay."

I told her we'd be home and would eagerly await the arrival of her famous pimiento cheese.

"I'm glad you're back to being a Baptist," Mary Lou said. "We've missed you. I can't wait till you join the church again and make it official."

"Oh, I never officially left," I said. "I guess the Lord knew He was going to need me back with the Baptists."

Mary Lou chuckled and hugged me goodbye. "Oh, Brenda," she said. Sometimes, I almost felt that Mary Lou was just a little bit condescending to me for some strange reason.

But then again, I always kept my opinions about such things to myself. Especially at Christmas.

A Year of Teatime Tales

51
Tea on Christmas Morning

Mary woke at five a.m., just as she did almost every day of the year. Bill was still fast asleep, so she reached for the worn burgundy leather Bible on her nightstand and quietly headed up the hall and into the den.

With her new red velvet ballet slippers warming her cold feet, she went to the kitchen and filled the electric teakettle with fresh water. It was a tradition of hers, beginning Christmas Day with a cup of tea and God.

For some thirty years, she'd been adding pieces to the same Christmas pattern she had started collecting as a young bride. The warm ivory tones and the cheerful Christmas tree design always brought a smile to her face. After steeping a cup of her favorite peppermint-flavored black tea, she headed to the sofa, spread a fluffy green Christmas throw over her lap, and opened her Bible to the second chapter of Luke. She read the familiar words as she sipped her tea.

And it came to pass in those days, that there went out a decree from Caesar Augustus, that all the world should be taxed. (And this taxing was first made when Cyrenius was governor of Syria.) And all went to be taxed, every one into his own city. And Joseph also went up from Galilee, out of the city of Nazareth, into Judaea, unto the city of David, which is called Bethlehem; (because he was of the house and lineage of David:) To be taxed with Mary his espoused wife, being great with child. And so it was, that, while they were there, the days were accomplished that she should be delivered. And she brought forth her firstborn son, and wrapped him in swaddling clothes, and laid him in a manger; because there was no room for them in the inn. And there were in the same country shepherds abiding in the field, keeping watch over their flock by night. And, lo, the angel of the Lord came upon them, and the glory of the Lord shone round about them: and they were sore afraid. And the angel said unto them, Fear not: for, behold, I bring you good tidings of great joy, which shall be to all people. For unto you is born this day in the city of David a Saviour, which is Christ the Lord.

Syria. Taxes. Fear. And courage. The topics were just as relevant two thousand years later, Mary thought. But she pushed all the recent news headlines out of her mind and tried, as she often did at Christmastime, to focus her wayward thoughts on the life-changing gift of the Christ child.

Earlier that week, she'd reread a favorite piece by a favorite author, Max Lucado, in which he'd pondered "Twenty-five Questions for Mary." He meant the other Mary, of course, but she always chose to imagine Max had intended the questions for her too.

Her favorite was the one that read: "Did you ever think, *That's God eating my soup?*" So practical, yet so thought-provoking. And like Max, Mary wondered if Mother-of-Jesus

Mary thought about the food she was serving to the son who was also her savior.

Mary ran her hand along the well-marked Bible passage and read again the words she so delighted in: *"For unto you is born this day in the city of David a Saviour, which is Christ the Lord."* And then she whispered, *Thank you, Lord.*

Snuggling beneath her green throw, Mary took a sip of tea and stared at the amber brew. She knew she had a full day ahead. In a few minutes, she would put the ham in the oven to bake. Then, she'd throw a few things in the crockpot to have appetizers ready when the family showed up at lunchtime. Her daughters and daughter-in-law would help with the casseroles and vegetables, and then they would open presents together before enjoying their traditional Christmas dinner.

After their meal, in another family tradition, Bill would pull out his old black leather Bible and share the Christmas story with the family members gathered around the table. Mary thought about how even the children liked to hear that amazing story each year, especially when Bill read it in what one of their grandsons called "his Bible voice."

Finishing her peppermint tea, Mary let her eyes scroll again through the passage in Luke. How fortunate she was to live in a day when her Messiah had already come, had already offered her the magnificent gift of eternal life.

She knew that later that day, she was likely to open gifts that brought her much pleasure. A new bathrobe, perhaps, or a teacup or two for her collection. The grandchildren might give her a new photo book for the year—always a favorite gift—and Bill might surprise her with that new electric teakettle she'd been hinting she would like.

And however her Christmas Day ended, she knew nothing would top the fact that it began, just as always, with good tidings of great joy.

52
A Year of Teatime

December 31, 3 p.m.

Dear Journal,

    I'm not sure I should tell Rick about my latest dream. Ever since Katie and Josh gave me that Old Country Roses tea set for Christmas last year, I seem to have been on a real tea kick, going to tearooms, shopping for teawares, and sipping more cups of tea than ever before in my life. I can't help believing that's one reason tea has been a part of my dreams on quite a few nights this year.
    Thank goodness I've made a habit of writing them down, because otherwise I'd never have recalled all those odd tea dreams of the past year. I remember having that first dream where my teacups were jealous of each other. At least that

one made me conscious of switching out my teacups and not using the same old ones over and over.

Then around St. Patrick's Day, I had that vivid dream about leprechauns magically disguising themselves on teacups and traveling to America from Ireland. How bizarre! And just this fall, after I visited Florida and took granddaughter Olivia to see *Cinderella* at the movies, I dreamed about going to an antiques shop where I spotted a poor but beautiful forgotten teapot and her ugly teapot stepsisters.

I can't believe that when I told Rick about that one, he gently suggested, "Marsha, maybe you need to collect something else — like first edition books." Sourpuss.

I have to say, though, that I was more than a little pleased when I got that new Old Country Roses casual style teapot from Katie, Josh, and the children on Christmas day. And of all things, that night, I dreamed that I wrote a book that included all these strange tea tales. Like anyone would ever read such a thing ...

Still, I'm glad my daughter's family got me hooked on collecting teawares, and they have certainly gotten me addicted to "all this tea stuff," as Rick puts it. He's just saying that because now I've gotten our granddaughter hooked on teatime too.

Just as she usually does, Katie arrived early for Christmas, and I was thrilled to have her here, but I was especially delighted to have our adorable grandchildren, Olivia and Ethan. I can't believe Olivia is three. And it seems like only yesterday I was headed down to Florida and Katie was giving birth to baby Ethan. Five months old, already!

I'm not sure I'll ever understand exactly what Josh does for a living there in Florida—something to do with cyber security—and why he has to come up later in December, but I don't mind having some quality time with Katie before her husband gets here.

On Christmas Eve, Rick and I gave Olivia a cute little tin tea set in a cardboard case, and after she opened it, she and I had tea together every day until they left. I do enjoy my loose leaf teas, but I don't think I've ever had any tea I enjoyed more than those pretend cups of tea—just regular tap water—I had with Olivia.

This Christmas, my heart has been so full. Really, my whole year has been. As I look back at my entries from January, I see I'd forgotten how worried I was about everything. I was worried about the new baby coming. I was worried about not having a long enough list of New Year's Resolutions. I was worried that I worried too much. Who *was* that woman? I don't miss her.

Looking back to one year ago, I think Rick and Katie were right when they said I worried too much. I gave up thinking life is all about racking up accomplishments, and while I haven't quite conquered all my Type A tendencies, I do think I'm much better about letting things go. Don't you, Journal Dear?

I mean, I no longer harp on Rick about all those ballgames he watches at this time of year. (Plus, I don't want him harping on me about all the tearooms I've started visiting.)

I didn't worry about whether or not I got my two-mile walk in every single day. (And interestingly enough, I'm ending the year ten pounds lighter. Go figure.)

I see I had also vowed not to worry about whether Josh could afford for his wife to be a stay-at-home mom. Whatever his job is, he must be good at it, because he got a promotion, and they bought a new SUV right before the baby was born.

So I think I'm probably through making lists of anxiety-producing New Year's Resolutions, and I'm going to stick with my goal of not worrying about things. Life was so much easier this year.

Besides, I like what the pastor said on Sunday about how worrying means we're having "faith in the negative." I've always said I put my faith in God, and it's time I started living like it.

Finally, Dear Journal, one thing I absolutely do not intend to worry over in the coming year is my newfound passion for teatime. I think I have had some sort of teatime almost every single day of the past year! I always thought teatime had to be a big production with invitations and a guest list. I've had some of those, sure, but some of my best teatimes were those quiet moments in the afternoon that I spent with a cup of hot tea, enjoying a book (or writing in this Journal), all by myself. I predict that's a tradition that will continue for many, many years to come.

So thank you, Dear Journal, for joining me on this journey for the past year, and since you've still got a few more blank pages inside, I'll see you in the new year too!

Love,

Marsha

www.ingramcontent.com/pod-product-compliance
Lightning Source LLC
Chambersburg PA
CBHW071911290426
44110CB00013B/1352